Reasoning Olympiad

Class 06

A must have book for all
Olympiads & Talent Search Exams...

by
Amogh Goyal

BLOOM CAP
Bloom Cap Edu Ventures Pvt. Ltd.

Bloom Cap Edu Ventures Pvt. Ltd.

卐 **Administrative & Production Office**

'Ramchhaya' 4577/15, Agarwal Road, Darya Ganj, New Delhi -110002
Tele: 011- 47630600, 43518550

卐 **ISBN:** 978-93-25519-05-3

卐 **PRICE:** ₹100.00

卐 **PO No :** TXT-XX-XXXXXXX-X-XX

For further information about the books log on to
www.bloomcap.org

Follow us on   

Preface

"Future belongs to those Who prepares for it today"

School Olympiads are National & International level competitions conducted by different Government, Non-Government & Educational Organisations with the purpose of making the children ready to face competitive exams. The challenging Questions asked in Olympiads motivate them to learn more & more and bring out the best result with improved academic performance. The Awards & Scholarship offered by Olympiads motivate children to aspire & strive for doing better and emerge out to be the best.

Reasoning Olympiads

Reasoning or Logical thinking is the ability of mind that helps in dealing with complex situations. It is also directly related to evolving careers like Software Development, Coding, Mobile App Development etc.

Reasoning Olympiads are targeted to induce & enhance the logical thinking skills and Analytical Approach in students which further aid to improve their academics.

'Bloom Reasoning Olympiad Study Book Class 6' is a perfect resource to Study & Practice for Olympiad Exams and other National & State Level Talent Search Exams & Other Competitions.

Some Special Features of Bloom Reasoning Olympiad Study Books are;

- Complete coverage of all the aspects of Reasoning; Verbal, Non-Verbal, Analytical & Logical Reasoning etc.
- Chapterwise Exercises having different types of Objective Questions at par with the Olympiad Level.
- Detailed Explanation for each question.
- Olympiad Pattern Practice Sets at the end.

This book is prepared by Expert Panel with the utmost care, still if you have any suggestions regarding its improvement then feel free to contact us at olympiads@bloomcap.org. We will try to inculcate your suggestions in the further editions.

Contents

Matching Pairs

'Matching pairs' are the pairs in which some relationship exist between the two elements of a pair and same relationship exists between the two elements of other pair.

Problems based on matching pair can be broadly classified into the following five categories.

1. Number Based

Number based analogy can be asked on the basis of addition, subtraction, multiply, division, square, cube of numbers.

EXAMPLE 1 18 is related to 36, in the same way as 21 is related to

(a) 63 (b) 42 (c) 12 (d) 40

Sol. (b) As, $18 \times 2 = 36$

Similarly, $21 \times 2 = \boxed{42}$

Hence, option (b) is correct.

2. Alphabet Based

Alphabet based analogy can be asked by following a series, skipping and opposites of alphabets.

Following letters position table in English alphabetical series will help the students to solve these type of questions.

Forward of Alphabetical Order

A	B	C	D	E	F	G	H	I	J	K	L	M	N	O	P	Q	R	S	T	U	V	W	X	Y	Z
1	2	3	4	5	6	7	8	9	10	11	12	13	14	15	16	17	18	19	20	21	22	23	24	25	26

Reverse Alphabetical Order

Z	Y	X	W	V	U	T	S	R	Q	P	O	N	M	L	K	J	I	H	G	F	E	D	C	B	A
26	25	24	23	22	21	20	19	18	17	16	15	14	13	12	11	10	9	8	7	6	5	4	3	2	1

EXAMPLE 2 Choose the one which completes the second pair in the same way as the first pair?

PAIN : KZRM : : STAR : ?

(a) TUBS (b) HGZI (c) UVCT (d) HGIZ

Sol. (b)

As, P A I N → K Z R M Similarly, S T A R → H G Z I

(Letters at the same position in reverse alphabetical series)

Here, we can see that each letter has letter which is exactly at the same position in reverse alphabetical series.

Hence, option (b) is the correct answer.

3. Word Based

This type of questions is based on the colour, position, shape, area, volume, vocabulary etc.

EXAMPLE 3 Petal : Flower : : ? : ?

(a) Salt : Pepper

(b) Tyre : Bicycle

(c) Base : Ball

(d) Puppy : Dog

Sol. (b) As petal is a part of flower. Similarly, tyre is a part of bicycle.

Hence, option (b) is correct.

4. Picture/Figure Based

Picture based analogy can be asked on the basis of rotation, elements relationship between the pair and geometrical shapes etc.

EXAMPLE 4 Consider the following pairs of figures and find out the missing figure.

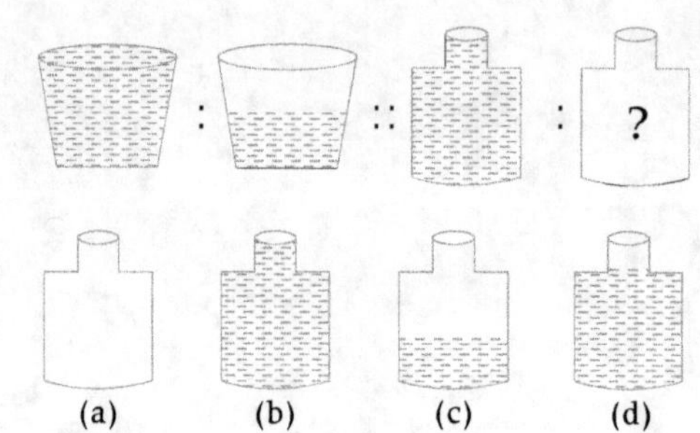

Sol. (c) Here, we see that in first pair a glass filled upto the brim becomes half and similarly in second pair bottle filled upto brim will become half.

So, option figure (c) will complete the second pair.

Hence, option (c) is correct.

5. Mixed Based

In such type of problems we deal with the questions with letters, numbers, figures, pictures all together.

EXAMPLE 7 Which will complete the second pair in the similar way as first pair?

△ : 27 :: □ : ?

(a) 64 (b) 8

(c) 4 (d) 256

Sol. (d) As, we have given here a triangle,

Total number of sides in a triangle = 3

$\therefore \quad (3)^3 = 27$

Similarly,

Total number of sides in a square = 4

$\therefore \quad 4^4 = \boxed{256}$

Hence, option (d) is the correct answer.

Let's Practice

1 Mark Questions

Directions (Q. Nos. 1 and 2) Find the matching pair of the following.

1. 186 is related to 3, in the same way as 6513 is related to
   (a) 6 (b) 7 (c) 4 (d) 5

2. 4 is to 9, as 7 is to
   (a) 13 (b) 14 (c) 15 (d) 16

Directions (Q. Nos. 3 and 4) Choose the one which completes the second pair in the same way as the first pair.

3. 6248 : 3124 : : 4024 : ?
   (a) 2102 (b) 2201 (c) 2012 (d) 2210

4. 423539 : 422539 : : 253682 : ?
   (a) 251682 (b) 252682
   (c) 252692 (d) 256282

Directions (Q. Nos. 5 and 6) Choose the one which completes the second pair in the same way as the first pair.

5. XW : ZY : : DJ : ?
   (a) FK (b) EL (c) FL (d) LF

6. ABC : BDF : : ? : MOM
   (a) LMJ (b) LML (c) LMN (d) LNJ

Directions (Q.Nos. 7 and 8) Find the matching pairs of the following.

7. KLM is related to MLK, in the same way HIJ is related to
   (a) JIH (b) IJH (c) IHJ (d) HJI

8. PNGRS is to RRINU as GPDCM is to?
   (a) ICPFO (b) ICFPO
   (c) CIFOP (d) CIPFO

Directions (Q. Nos. 9 and 10) Choose the one which completes the second pair in the same way as the first pair.

9. Helicopter : Aircraft : : Almond : ?
   (a) Expensive (b) Nut
   (c) Fruit (d) Cashew

10. Peacock : India : : Kangaroo : ?
   (a) Russia (b) England
   (c) Australia (d) America

Directions (Q. Nos. 11 and 12) In each of the following questions, a pair of words is given. From amongst the four given alternatives, choose the pair which shows a relationship similar to the one expressed in the given pair.

11. Car : Automobile
   (a) Paper : Book (b) Vegetable : Potato
   (c) Cat : Animal (d) Game : Soccer

12. Mother : Parent
   (a) Uncle : Nephew
   (b) Sister : Sibling
   (c) Father : Son
   (d) Daughter : Sister

Directions (Q. Nos. 13-15) Which figure/pattern completes the second pair in the same way as the first pair?

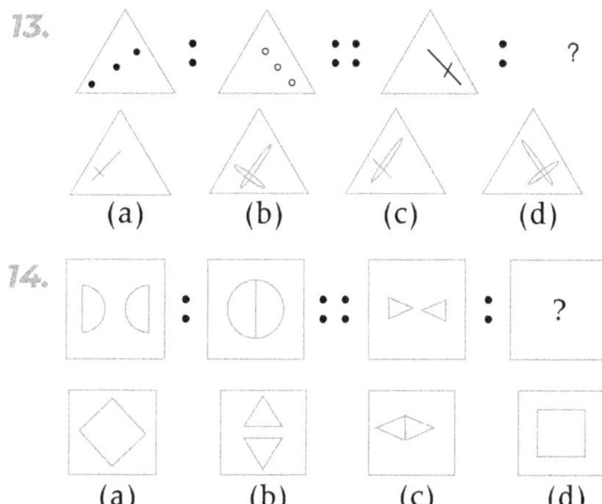

15. Choose the pair which shows a relationship similar to the one expressed in the given pair.

G*M : 7*13

(a) B*D : 4*2 (b) L*O : 11*15
(c) X*F : 25*6 (d) P*T : 16*20

16. BD is related to 6, in the same way LK is related to

(a) 22
(b) 23
(c) 24
(d) 25

2 Marks Questions

17. Find the missing term.

542 : 245 | 368 : 863 | 929 : ?

(a) 928 (b) 929 (c) 930 (d) 939

18. Choose the pair which shows a relationship similar to the one expressed in the given pair.

CARE : HFWJ

(a) BOSS : GTXY (b) CROP : HXTU
(c) GOAL : LTFQ (d) FEEL : KJKQ

19. GREAT is to SHUYF as WORLD is to?

(a) HVNCK (b) CKNVH
(c) CKHNV (d) NVHCK

20. Find the missing term.

AB : 3 | CD : 7 | EF : ?

(a) 11 (b) 10 (c) 12 (d) 9

21. Select a suitable figure from the answer figures that would replace the question mark (?).

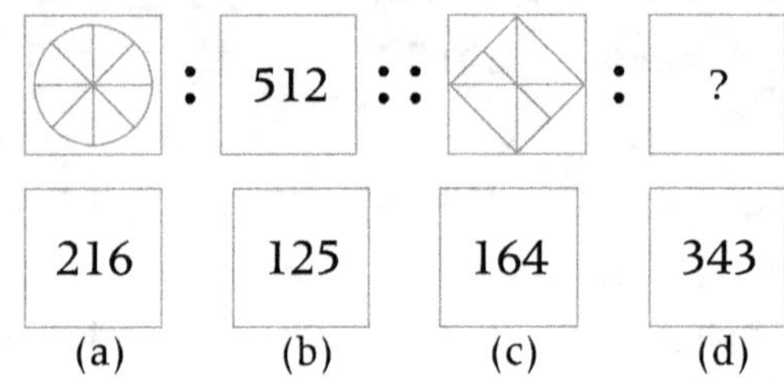

22. Find the missing term.

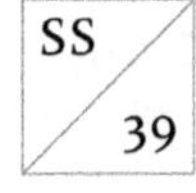

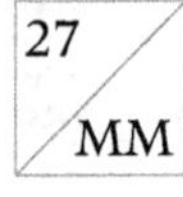

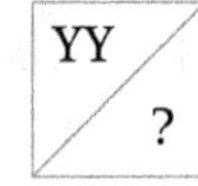

(a) 61 (b) 51 (c) 48 (d) 44

23. Select a suitable figure from the answer figures that would replace the question mark.

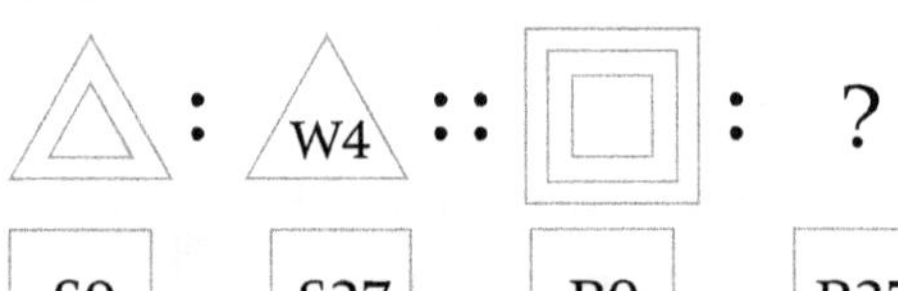

(a) S9 (b) S27 (c) R9 (d) R27

Chapter 02

Odd One Out

In 'Odd One Out', a group of some items is given. All these items, except one are similar in a certain way.

The students are required to spot out this odd item, i.e. the one which does not fit into the given group of items.

Problem based on Odd one out can be broadly classified into the following five categories.

1. Alphabet Based

In this type of questions alphabets showing different features will be odd one out.

EXAMPLE 1 Find the odd one among the following.

(a) ARQ
(b) IKJ
(c) TUV
(d) FHG

Sol. (d) Except FHG, there is a vowel in all the other letter groups but in FHG, all the three letters are consonants.

2. Number Based

In this type of questions, students are asked to find the odd one on the basis of types of number, square root and cube root etc.

EXAMPLE 2 Choose the odd one out.

(a) 1024 (b) 1460
(c) 1998 (d) 2841

Sol. (a) Except 1024, all other numbers are not a perfect square of any number while 1024 is a perfect square of 32.

3. Word Based

In this type of questions, word having uncommon feature with respect to other than words is called odd word.

EXAMPLE 3 Choose odd one out?

(a) Euro (b) Dollar (c) Yen (d) Japan

Sol. (d) Except Japan, all are currencies of different countries while Japan is a country itself.

4. Picture Based

In this type of questions, student are asked to select the odd figure on the basis of some similar properties.

EXAMPLE 4 Choose a figure which is different from other.

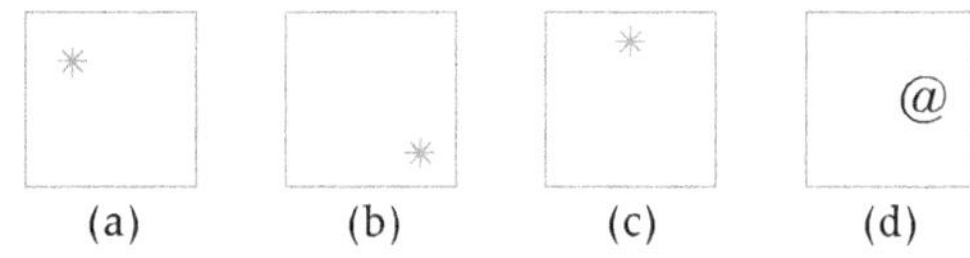

Sol. (d) All other squares have star point except in option (d). Hence, option (d) is different.

5. Mixed Based

This type of questions involves the usage of word, letters, symbols or their combination.

EXAMPLE 5 Choose the figure which is different from other?

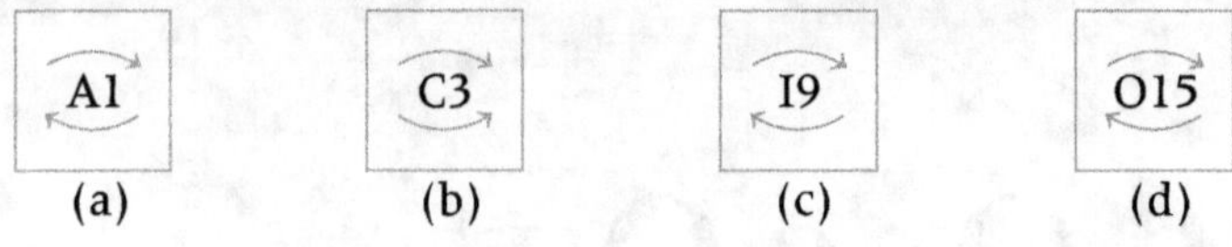

Sol. (b) Except option (b), all the figures have vowels along with their place value with two arrows moving in opposite directions. Hence, option (b) is different.

Let's Practice

1 Mark Questions

Directions (Q. Nos. 1-4) Identify the odd one out.

1\.
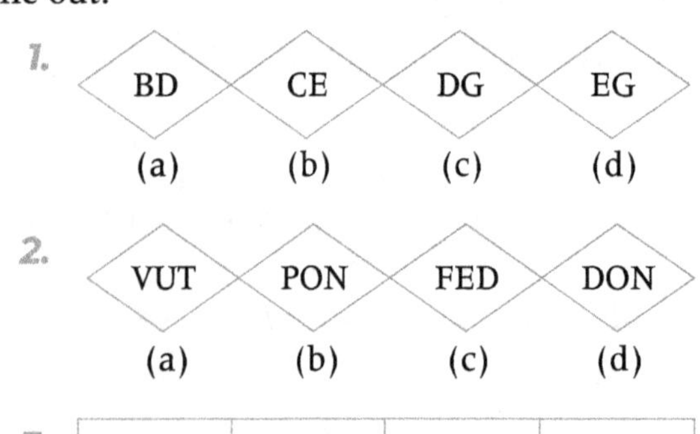

2\.

3\.

CDWX	EFVW	MNOP	IJRQ
(a)	(b)	(c)	(d)

Directions (Q. Nos. 4-6) Find the odd one out.

4\.
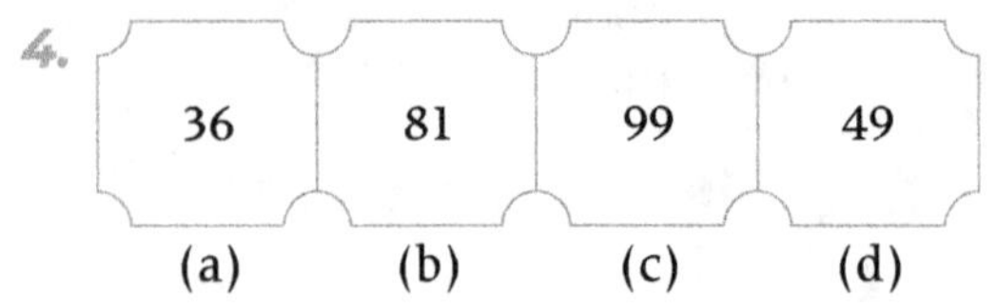

5\.
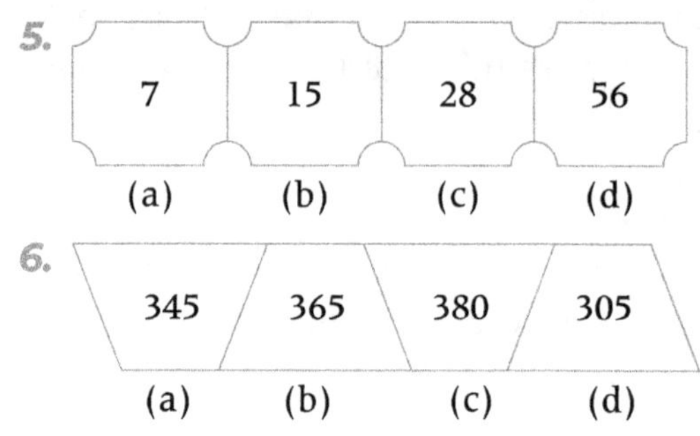

6\.

Directions (Q. Nos. 7-9) Choose the odd one out.

7\.

Nose	Lungs	Hand	Knee
(a)	(b)	(c)	(d)

8\.

Japan	Bhutan	Nepal	Beijing
(a)	(b)	(c)	(d)

9\.

Bus	Motor-cycle	Bicycle	Car
(a)	(b)	(c)	(d)

Directions (Q. Nos. 10 and 11) In each of the following questions, choose the odd one out.

10. 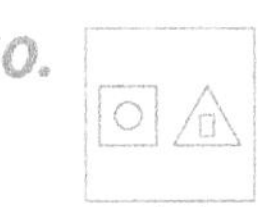 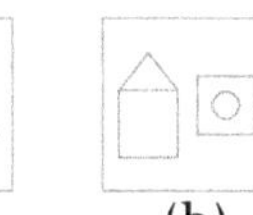 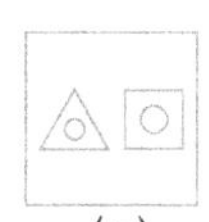 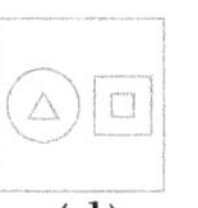
(a) (b) (c) (d)

11. 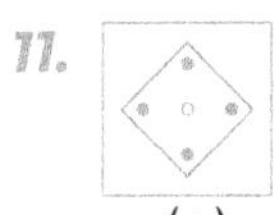 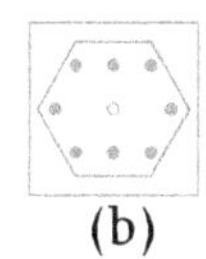
(a) (b) (c) (d)

Directions (Q. Nos. 12 and 13) Find odd one out of the following.

12. 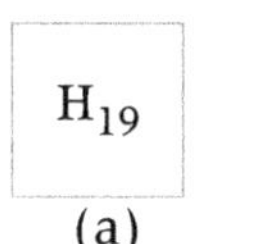

H_{19}	L_{15}	C_{23}	G_{26}
(a)	(b)	(c)	(d)

13. 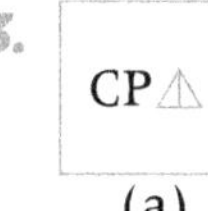 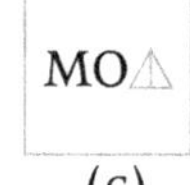

CP	DEM	MO	UX
(a)	(b)	(c)	(d)

2 Marks Questions

Directions (Q. Nos. 14-16) Find the odd one out of the following.

14.  
(a) (b) (c) (d)

15. 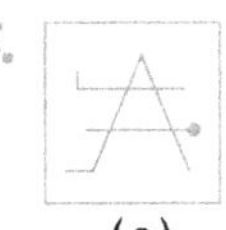 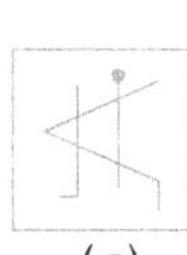
(a) (b) (c) (d)

16. 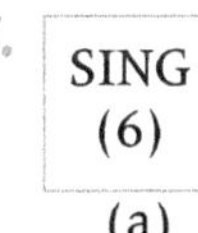

SING (6)	MAN (7)	DOLLS (7)	EAT (5)
(a)	(b)	(c)	(d)

17. Find the odd group of letters
(a) ABDE (b) FGIJ
(c) KLOP (d) QRTU

18. Find the odd one out.
(a) TuvL (b) IJKL (c) EfgH (d) PqrS

19. Find the odd one out.
(a) DEAR (b) NEAR
(c) BEAR (d) KEAR

20. Find the odd group of numbers.
(a) 25, 50, 56
(b) 20, 40, 46
(c) 18, 36, 40
(d) 12, 24, 30

21. Rearrange the jumbled alphabets in the following four options and find the odd one among them.
(a) RARCTO
(b) NIATCRU
(c) BACGEBA
(d) ILBJARN

Chapter 03

What Comes Next ?

'What Comes Next?' means finding the next term based on a given arrangement.

It is also known as 'Series'. Student's are required to analyse the pattern followed by series and find the next term.

Problems based on 'What Comes Next' can be classified into four categories.

1. Alphabet Based

In this type of questions a pattern is given which is based on the position of letters in English alphabetical series.

EXAMPLE 1 What comes next in the series given below?

(A) (B) (D) (G) (K) (?)

(a) P (b) Q (c) R (d) L

Sol. (a) The given series can be represented as

$$A \xrightarrow{+1} B \xrightarrow{+2} D \xrightarrow{+3} G \xrightarrow{+4} K \xrightarrow{+5} \boxed{P}$$

Here, each letter is 1, 2, 3, 4, ... steps ahead to its previous letter.

Therefore, the next letter will be K + 5 i.e. P, as shown above.

Hence, option (a) is correct.

2. Number Based

In this type of questions a pattern is given which is based on addition, subtraction, multiplication and division of numbers.

EXAMPLE 2 Complete the following series.

(a) 13 (b) 14 (c) 16 (d) 17

Sol. (d) In the given series, numbers are arranged in the following pattern

$$2 \xrightarrow{+1} 3 \xrightarrow{+2} 5 \xrightarrow{+3} 8 \xrightarrow{+4} 12 \xrightarrow{+5} \boxed{17}$$

Therefore, the next number will be 12 + 5 i.e. 17, as shown above.

Hence, option (d) is correct.

3. Picture Based

In this type of questions some figures/ shapes are arranged in a certain pattern.

EXAMPLE 3 Consider the following series of figures and find out the next figure.

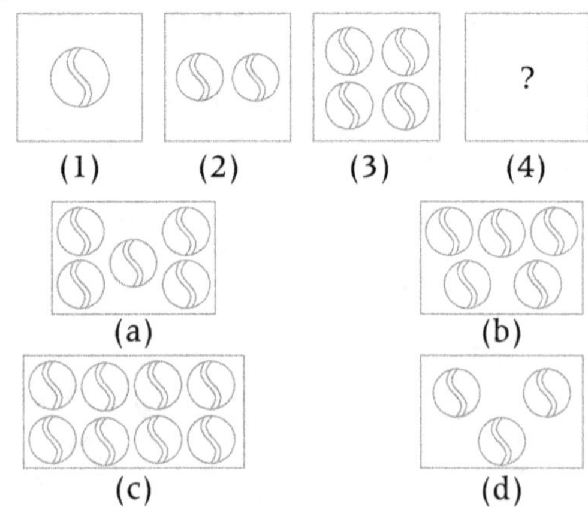

Sol. (c) The given series can be represented as

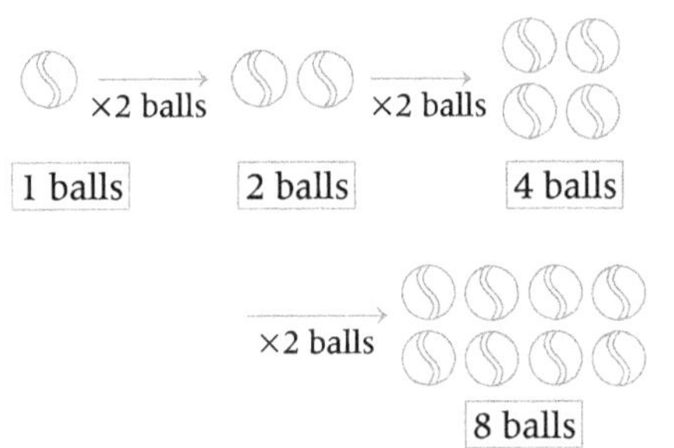

So, it will be $4 \times 2 = 8$ balls in the next step. Hence, option (c) is correct.

EXAMPLE 4 Find the next term for the series given below.

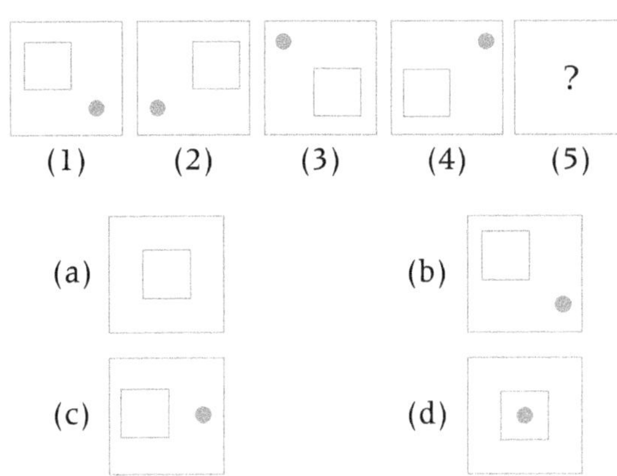

Sol. (b) The series can be represented as :

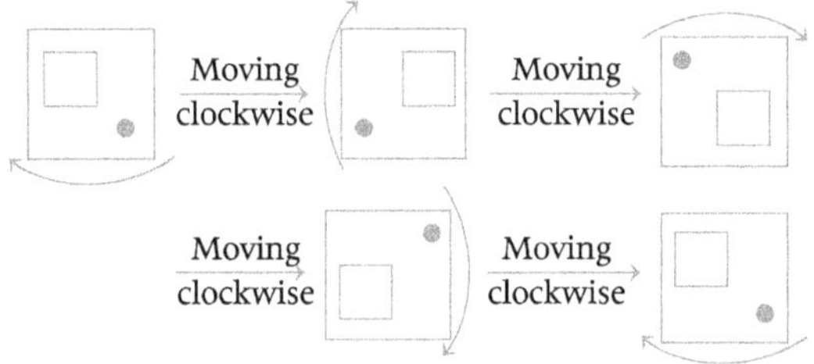

Therefore, option figure (b) will complete the series. Hence, option (b) is correct.

4. Alpha-Numeric Series

In alpha-numeric series, letters and numbers together are arranged in a specific pattern.

EXAMPLE 5 Find the next term in the given series.

AB3	DE9	GH15	?

(a) KJ12 (b) JK21
(c) JK12 (d) KJ21

Sol. (b) The pattern of the series is as follows:

$$A \xrightarrow{+3} D \xrightarrow{+3} G \xrightarrow{+3} \boxed{J}$$
$$B \xrightarrow{+3} E \xrightarrow{+3} H \xrightarrow{+3} \boxed{K}$$
$$3 \xrightarrow{+6} 9 \xrightarrow{+6} 15 \xrightarrow{+6} \boxed{21}$$

Hence, option (b) is correct.

Let's Practice

1 Mark Questions

Directions (Q. Nos.1-3) Find the next term in the given series.

1. 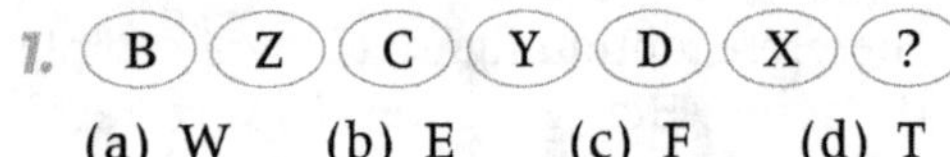

(a) W (b) E (c) F (d) T

2. 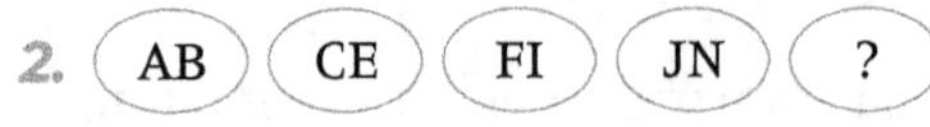

(a) TO (b) OS
(c) SO (d) OT

3. 

(a) LM (b) MO
(c) NO (d) KN

Directions (Q. Nos. 4 and 5) Find the two missing terms in the given boxes.

4.

BA	BA	CB	ED	HG	?	?

(a) KL, QP (b) LK, PQ
(c) LK, QP (d) KL, PQ

5.

HPW	IPS	JPO	KPK	?	?

(a) LPH, MPC (b) GPL, CPM
(c) LPG, MPC (d) MPC, LPH

Directions (Q. Nos. 6-11) Find the next/missing number in the given series.

6. 98 90 82 74 ?

(a) 70 (b) 60
(c) 69 (d) 66

7. 400 200 100 50 ?

(a) 25 (b) 40
(c) 15 (d) 30

8. 15 45 20 42 25 39 ?

(a) 36 (b) 30 (c) 25 (d) 40

9. 100 98 94 86 70 ?

(a) 83 (b) 07
(c) 38 (d) 89

10. 8 66 8 9 56 6 7 ? 5

(a) 35 (b) 34
(c) 37 (d) 44

11.

2004	2009	2016	?	2036	?	2064

(a) 2008, 2036 (b) 2001, 2010
(c) 2025, 2094 (d) 2025, 2049

Directions (Q. Nos. 12-15) Find the next figure in the series given below.

12. ?

(1) (2) (3) (4) (5)

(a) (b) (c) (d)

13. ?

(1) (2) (3) (4) (5)

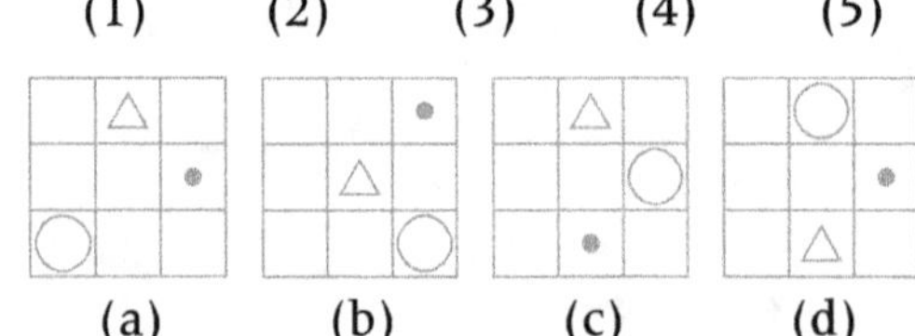

(a) (b) (c) (d)

14\.

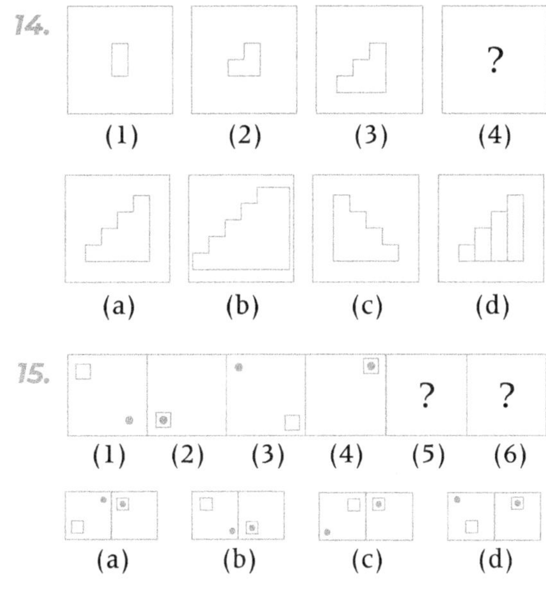

15\.

Direction (Q.No. 16) Select the figure from the options which will continue the same series as established by the problem figures.

16\.

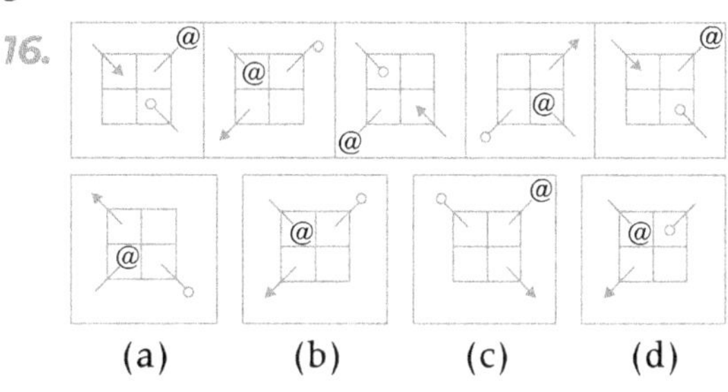

Directions (Q. Nos. 21 and 22) Find the next term in the given series.

17\. A01 B11 C21 D22 E23 F33 ?

(a) 34G (b) G34 (c) G31 (d) G30

18\. AB9 AC16 AD25 AE36 AF49 ?

(a) AG46 (b) AG50
(c) AG63 (d) AG64

2 Marks Questions

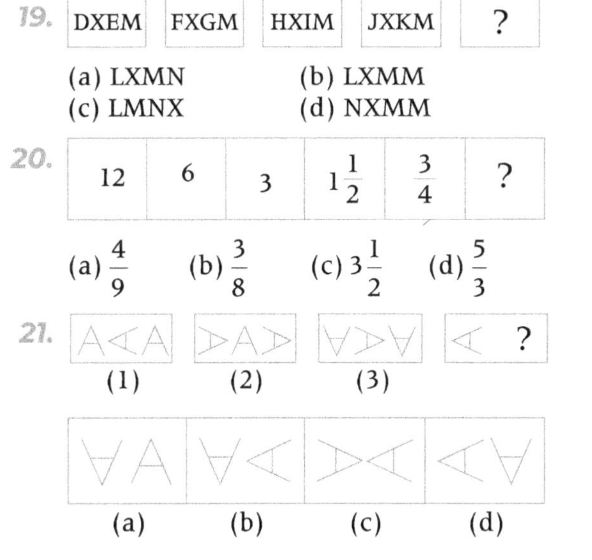

19\. DXEM FXGM HXIM JXKM ?

(a) LXMN (b) LXMM
(c) LMNX (d) NXMM

20\. 12 6 3 $1\frac{1}{2}$ $\frac{3}{4}$?

(a) $\frac{4}{9}$ (b) $\frac{3}{8}$ (c) $3\frac{1}{2}$ (d) $\frac{5}{3}$

21\.

22\.

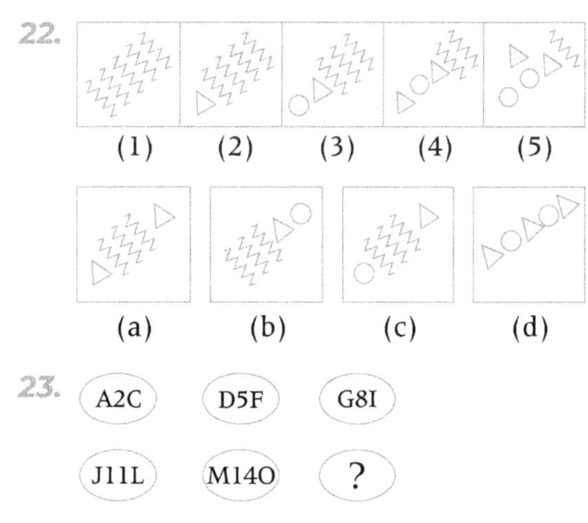

23\. A2C D5F G8I J11L M14O ?

(a) P17R (b) Q20S
(c) Q18S (d) S18Q

Chapter
04

Coding-Decoding

Coding is a method of conveying a message in secret way.

Decoding is a process to break the code to understand the conveyed message.

Problem based on the Coding-Decoding can be classified into five categories.

- Letter coding
- Number coding
- Substitution coding
- Sentence coding
- Symbol coding

1. Letter Coding

In such type of coding, letters are moved in forward backward or in both the directions according to the english alphabetical series.

EXAMPLE 1 In a certain code, GOAL is coded as HPBM, in the same way BEAR is coded as

(a) SBFC (b) FSBC
(c) CFBS (d) BFSC

Sol. (c) As,

G O A L
+1 +1 +1 +1
H P B M

Similarly,

B E A R
+1 +1 +1 +1
C F B S

Hence, option (c) is correct.

EXAMPLE 2 If in a certain code, CLOCK is coded as KCOLC, how is STEPS coded in that code?

(a) SPETS (b) SPSET
(c) SPEST (d) STEPS

Sol. (a) As,

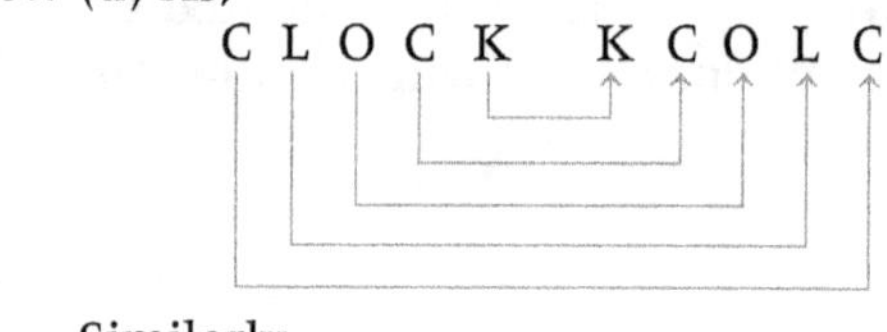

Similarly,

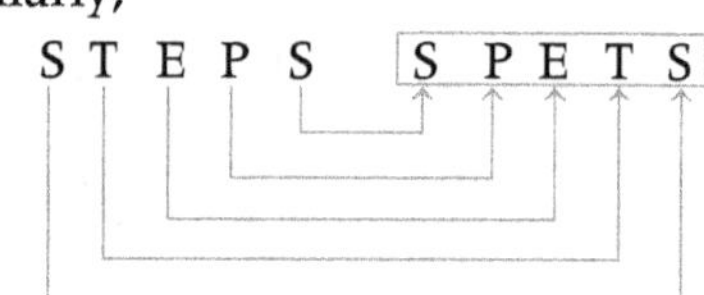

Hence, option (a) is correct.

2. Number Coding

In such type of coding sometimes numerical values are assigned to a letter or symbol or words.

EXAMPLE 3 In a certain code '35768' is written as 'CQTJO' and '2914' as 'LNMY' then which number will be written as 'MOCNJ'?

(a) 97253 (b) 18714
(c) 18396 (d) 97614

Sol. (c) We have some codes for these numbers.

3	5	7	6	8
C	Q	T	J	O

and

2	9	1	4
L	N	M	Y

From the both tables,
'MOCNJ' will be written as '18396'.
Hence, option (c) is correct.

3. Substitution Coding

In such type of coding sometimes some particular words are assigned to a certain name or word.

EXAMPLE 4 If blue is called red, red is called green, green is called yellow and yellow is called white, then the colour of grass is

(a) white
(b) yellow
(c) red
(d) blue

Sol. (b) We know that, the colour of grass is green, but in the given code, green is coded as yellow. So, the colour of grass is yellow. Hence, option (b) is correct.

4. Sentence Coding

In such type of coding two, three or more than three sentences are given in the coded language and the code for a particular word is asked. To find the code for the particular word, pickup two sentences bearing a common word and the common code will mean that word.

EXAMPLE 5 If in a certain code language, 'te ne' means 'good boy', 're ne se' means 'girls are good', 'he re na' means 'you are fool'. Then, find the code for 'girls' in that language.

(a) se (b) te (c) ne (d) re

Sol. (a)

te ne → good boy ... (i)

re ne se → girls are good ... (ii)

he re na → you are fool ... (iii)

From Eqs. (i) and (ii), we get
ne → good, te → boy
From Eqs. (ii) and (iii),
re → are, se → girls
So, the code for girls is 'se'.
Hence, option (a) is correct.

5. Symbol Coding

In this coding, we use the symbols like "!@#$%^&*+−()_" to represent words or letter.

These codes are used to determine a code for the given words/letters/numbers that are written down.

EXAMPLE 6 If "PXOM" is written as "@$%#", "EMRT" is written as "&?*^", then how "PROPER" is coded in the same way?

(a) @*%@&* (b) *@%@&*
(c) ?&^@@% (d) #*@%^?

Sol. (a) To solve these types of questions, a table may come in handy.

P	X	O	M
@	$	%	#

E	M	R	T
&	?	*	^

From the both tables,
'PROPER' is coded as '@*%@&*'
Hence option (a) is correct.

Let's Practice

1 Mark Questions

1. If HEALTH is coded as GDZKSG, then code for NORTH is
   (a) OPSUI (b) GSQNM
   (c) FRPML (d) MNQSG

2. If CORDIAL is coded as ENTCKZN, then code for SOMEDAY is
   (a) UNODFZA (b) TNECKZN
   (c) DFZANOU (d) DFZNOUA

3. In a certain code language MOCKS is written as 'NNDJT'. How is FLAME written in that language ?
   (a) KFBMA (b) GKBLF
   (c) LBHGK (d) LBGHG

4. If BAKE is coded as 5796 and FIRE is coded as 3146, then FEAR is coded as
   (a) 6374 (b) 3674
   (c) 4763 (d) 6347

5. In a certain code language, FRONT is written as 618151420 and BORNE is written as 21518145. How is MORNS written in that code language?
   (a) 1315181419 (b) 1314161718
   (c) 81291114 (d) 141154321

6. If A = 2 , D = 8, K = 22 and TEN = 78, then BEL is coded as
   (a) 83 (b) 39
   (c) 38 (d) 30

7. If 'SEASON' is coded as '50' and 'FOCUS' as '40', then what is the code for 'CHALLENGE'?
   (a) 80 (b) 90 (c) 60 (d) 70

8. If LAMP is coded as 30-52-28-22, then TOY will be coded as
   (a) 14-24-4 (b) 20-15-25
   (c) 14-4-24 (d) 20-25-15

9. If 'red' is called 'pink', 'pink' is called 'black', 'black' is called 'white' and 'white' is called 'blue', then colour of milk is
   (a) black (b) white
   (c) blue (d) pink

10. If 'water' is called 'food', 'food' is called 'tree', 'tree' is called 'sky', 'sky' is called 'wall', then on which of the following a fruit grows?
    (a) Water (b) Food
    (c) Sky (d) Tree

11. In a certain code language, '256' means 'you are good'. 637 means 'we are bad' and '358' means 'good and bad'. Which of the following represents 'and' in that code?
    (a) 2 (b) 5
    (c) 8 (d) 3

12. In a certain code language 'si# po@ re$' means 'effort is good' 'ti# na@ re$' means 'real is time' 'ka*si#' means 'interesting effort' and 'de$ ti#' means 'that real' which of the following means 'that is effort' in that code language?
    (a) de$ ti# re$ (b) de$ re$si#
    (c) po@ re$ ti# (d) si# po@ ti#

2 Marks Questions

Direction (Q. No. 13) In the following question, read the given information carefully and answer the questions

In a certain code meaning of some words are as follows.

(i) 'ho na ta' means 'food is good'.
(ii) 'sa ta la' means 'eat food regularly'.
(iii) 'da na ja' means 'keep good health'.

13. Which of the following means 'food' in that code language?
(a) la (b) ta (c) na (d) da

14. If RAID is written as % #©$ and RIPE is coded as %©@★, then DEAR is coded as
(a) $★#% (b) ★#%$
(c) $%★# (d) #%$★

Directions (Q.Nos. 15 and 16) The table given below given the codes for consonants of the English alphabets.

Letters	B	F	J	M	Q	T	X
	C	G	K	N	R	V	Y
	D	H	L	P	S	W	Z
Digits	7	6	2	1	5	8	9

Questions are based on the following conditions

(i) Letters of the english alphabets are coded by the digits given in the above table.
(ii) If any vowel is neither at the first place nor at the last place of the word then it is coded as '3'.
(iii) If any vowel is either at the first or at the last place of the word then both are coded as '4'.
(iv) If the same vowel is at the first and at the last place of the word then it is coded as '@'.

Applying these conditions find the right code in each questions.

15. Find the code for the word 'SOLUTION'.
(a) 23383315 (b) 53238331
(c) 53283331 (d) 33331528

16. Find the code for the word 'ENCOURAGE'.
(a) @7133536@ (b) @@1733536
(c) @1733536@ (d) @17@33356

Directions (Q. NOs. 17 and 18) Study the following information carefully to answer the given questions.

In a certain code language

'Plot for all persons' is written as 'fn bo dl sw'
'find the hidden plot' is written as 'dl et ga nu'
'try and find out' is written as 'ga yc mp zh'
'for the lock out' is written as 'nu mp fn rv'
(All codes are two letter codes only)

17. If 'try the key' is coded as 'nu ka yc', in the given code language, then how will 'key and lock' be coded as?
(a) ka bo zh (b) zh ga ka
(c) ka zh rv (d) bo rv ga

18. In the given code language, what does the code 'sw' stand for?
(a) either 'for' or 'find'
(b) either 'persons' or 'all'
(c) hidden
(d) for

Alphabet and Number Test

Alphabet Test

In such type of problems, a letter of the English alphabet is given and it is asked to determine the letter that is placed at a certain positions to the left/right of the given letter. Before moving forward, let us revise the positional values of each of the letters in the English alphabet.

Forward Alphabetical Order

A	B	C	D	E	F	G	H	I	J	K	L	M	N	O	P	Q	R	S	T	U	V	W	X	Y	Z
1	2	3	4	5	6	7	8	9	10	11	12	13	14	15	16	17	18	19	20	21	22	23	24	25	26

Reverse Alphabetical Order

Z	Y	X	W	V	U	T	S	R	Q	P	O	N	M	L	K	J	I	H	G	F	E	D	C	B	A
26	25	24	23	22	21	20	19	18	17	16	15	14	13	12	11	10	9	8	7	6	5	4	3	2	1

EXAMPLE 1 Which letter is fourth to the right of M in English alphabetical order?

(a) Q (b) O (c) P (d) R

Sol. (a) As it can be seen from the above table (alphabetical order), the position of M in the English alphabet is 13. Fourth to the right of M means (13 + 4), i.e., 17th position.

Clearly, the letter Q is present at the 17th position. Thus, the letter fourth to the right of M is Q.

Hence, option (a) is correct.

Problems based on 'Alphabet and Number Test' are broadly classified into four categories.

1. Word Formation Test

In such type of problems a word is given and you have to find out the number of words that can be formed out of given letters of that particular word.

EXAMPLE 2 Some letters are given which numbered 1, 2, 3, 4, 5 and 6 followed by four options containing combinations of these numbers. Find the combination such that letters when arranged accordingly form meaningful word.

T	R	E	H	F	A
1	2	3	4	5	6

(a) 436215 (b) 561432
(c) 632145 (d) 213645

Sol. (b) Meaningful word formed by the letter

561432 → FATHER

Hence, option (b) is correct.

2. Sequence of Words

In logical sequence of words, a group of words is given and students are required to arrange these words in a meaningful or logical order.

EXAMPLE 3 Arrange the words in a meaningful/logical order and then select the appropriate sequence from the alternatives given below:

1. Thousand 2. Trillion
3. Billion 4. Hundred

(a) 4, 3, 2, 1 (b) 4, 1, 3, 2
(c) 3, 2, 4, 1 (d) 2, 3, 1, 4

Sol. (b) The words can be arranged in meaningful and logical order as shown below

Hundred → Thousand → Billion → Trillion
i.e., 4, 1, 3, 2

Hence, option (b) is correct.

3. Word Cannot be Formed

In this type of questions, a word is given, followed by four other words. You have to identify the word which cannot be formed by using the letters of given word.

EXAMPLE 4 Select the word from the given alternatives which cannot be formed using the letters of the given word.
"DISTANCE"

(a) TENS (b) STAND
(c) DANCE (d) TEASE

Sol. (d) In the word 'DISTANCE' there is only one 'E' present but in the word 'TEASE' we need two 'E' letters. So, TEASE cannot be formed. Hence, option (d) is correct.

4. Alpha-Numeric Sequence Test

In such type of problems, a sequence of letters and numbers is given in jumbled form and the students are required to count the number of occurrences of a particular letter/number following a certain rule (condition).

EXAMPLE 5 Which of the following would be the 4th element to the right of the 13th element from the left end?
8 C M @ N £ T 2 4 γ 6 5 £ Q $ 7 ★ W # Z

(a) # (b) W (c) £ (d) ★

Sol. (d) 13th element from the left is '£' and 4th element to the right of '£' is '★'.

5. Number Test

In number test, a numerical sequence is given that follows a logical rule. Here, students are required to find the numbers based on the given situation asked in question.

EXAMPLE 6 In the following sequence, find out the number of the 3's, which are neither preceded by 6 nor immediately followed by 9.

9 3 6 6 3 9 5 9 3 7 8 9 1 6 3 9 6 3 9

(a) 3 (b) 2 (c) 4 (d) 1

Sol. (b) Here, in the above sequence there are two 3's, which are neither preceded by 6 nor immediately followed by 9 as shown below:

9 [3] 6 6 3 9 5 9 [3] 7 8 9 1 6 3 9 6 3 9

Hence, option (b) is correct.

Let's Practice

1 Mark Questions

1. Which letter is sixth to the left of 'O' in English alphabetical order?
(a) F (b) U
(c) I (d) J

2. Find the 9th letter to the left of 14th letter from the right in the English alphabetical order?
(a) B (b) D
(c) E (d) U

3. Which letter is in middle between the 9th letter from the right and eighth letter from the left in the English alphabetical order?
(a) N (b) M
(c) P (d) O

Directions (Q.Nos. 4 and 5) Read the following information carefully and answer the questions are based on the following alphabet series.

A B C D E F G H I J K L M N O P Q R S T U V W X Y Z

4. If the above alphabets are written in the reverse order, which letter will be twelfth to the left of the sixteenth letter from your left?
(a) D (b) V (c) W (d) X

5. Which letter is thirteenth from the right end if the alphabet series is reversed?
(a) M (b) R
(c) P (d) S

Direction (Q. No. 6) In each of the following questions, a group of letters is given which are numbered 1, 2, 3, 4 and 5. Select from the four alternatives containing the combinations of these numbers, to form a meaningful word.

6. N A E H L D
1 2 3 4 5 6
(a) 2, 6, 4, 3, 5, 1 (b) 4, 2, 1, 6, 5, 3
(c) 4, 3, 6, 5, 2, 1 (d) 2, 1, 6, 4, 3, 5

Directions (Q. Nos. 7 and 8) In each of the following questions a word is given, followed by four other words, one of which can be formed by using the letters of given word, then find that word.

7. MEASURE
(a) SURG (b) SAME
(c) MOON (d) READ

8. CORRESPONDING
(a) REPENT
(b) DISCERN
(c) CORRECT
(d) PANDINEG

Directions (Q. Nos. 9 and 10) In each of the following questions a word is given followed by four other words, one of which one word cannot be formed by using the letters of given word. Find that particular word.

9. REPUTATION
(a) TUTOR (b) PONTER
(c) RETIRE (d) EAT

10. PORTFOLIO
(a) RIFT (b) ROOF
(c) FORT (d) FORM

11. How many such letters are there in the word 'CATEGORY', which remains same in its position, when they are arrange in alphabetical order?
(a) One (b) Two
(c) Three (d) More than three

Directions (Q. Nos. 12 and 13) In each of the following questions, arrange the words in a meaningful and logical order and then select the appropriate sequence from the alternatives provided below.

12. 1. Table 2. Wood 3. Tree 4. Plant 5. Seed
(a) 4, 5, 3, 2, 1
(b) 5, 4, 3, 2, 1
(c) 1, 3, 2, 4, 5
(d) 1, 2, 3, 5, 4

13. 1. Leaves 2. Branch 3. Flower 4. Tree 5. Fruit
(a) 12345 (b) 35412
(c) 54321 (d) 42135

14. Which of the following word will come first, if all of these are arranged alphabetically as in a dictionary?
(a) Wasp (b) Waste (c) Wrist (d) War

15. Which of the following element is fourth from the left end in the series?

4 K Z R T 3 P 8 A X D 2 I Q 4 M

(a) T (b) I (c) 3 (d) R

16. In the given sequence of letters, how many T's are preceded and followed by Q?

QTQTTQQTQTTQQQTTQQTTQQQT

(a) Zero (b) One (c) Two (d) Three

2 Marks Questions

Directions (Q. Nos. 17 and 18) Study the following number sequence given below and answer the question.

8 9 7 6 3 4 2 8 9 7 6 4 5 9 2 9 7

17. How many 7's are preceded by 9 and followed by 6?
(a) 2 (b) 3
(c) 4 (d) 5

18. How many 9's are there which are preceded by even numbers?
(a) 1 (b) 4
(c) 2 (d) 3

19. How many meaningful English words can be formed with the letters 'ESTR', using each letter only once in each word?
(a) One (b) Two
(c) Three (d) None

20. If in the following group of words, first and last alphabets are interchanged, then which one of following word starts with vowel?

MAP QPU STF SJM

(a) MAP (b) QPU (c) STI (d) SJM

21. How many vowels in the given sequence are preceded by a symbol?
A @ 5 8 J N & E * # U 1 % T Q J 8
(a) One (b) Two
(c) Three (d) None of these

22. If in the following numbers, first and last digits are interchanged, then which one of the following will be the least number?

319, 409, 418, 719

(a) 319 (b) 409 (c) 418 (d) 719

23. How many such digits are there in the number '984667325' which remains in its position, when they are arranged in descending order from left to right?
(a) One (b) Two (c) Three (d) None

Ranking Test

In such type of problems, the rank (position) of a person from the top and bottom (from the left and right) is given and it is asked to determine the total number of persons.

In another variant, the total number of persons and the rank of a person from one of the ends is given, it is asked to determine the rank of the person from the other end.

EXAMPLE 1 In a class of 25 students, if Ram's rank is 16th from the bottom, then what is his rank from the top?

(a) 13th (b) 10th (c) 9th (d) 11th

Sol. (b) According to the question,

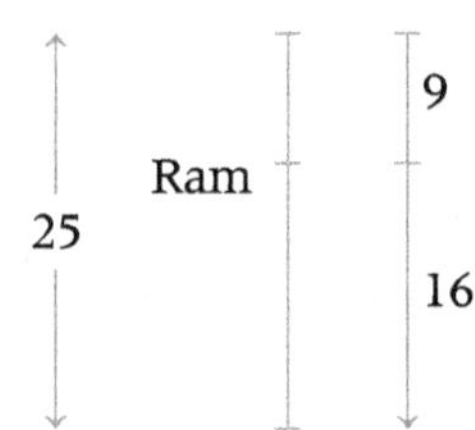

$\therefore$ Number of students at top of Ram $= 25 - 16 = 9$.

Now, position of Ram from top $= 9 +$ Ram itself $= 9 + 1 = 10$ th

Hence, option (b) is correct.

EXAMPLE 2 The strength of a class is 35. From the bottom, the position of Samyak is 7th and Rahul is placed at 9th from the top. Mayank is present at the middle position in between Samyak and Rahul. Determine the position of Samyak from Mayank.

(a) 9 (b) 10 (c) 11 (d) 13

Sol. (b) Total number of students present between Samyak and Rahul $= 35 - (7 + 9) = 17$

Middle of 17 is 9th position.

So, Samyak is 9th position above Mayank or his position is 10th.

Let's Practice

1 Mark Questions

1. Sohan ranks 7th from the top and 26th form the bottom in a class. How many students are there in the class?
   (a) 31 (b) 32
   (c) 34 (d) 33

2. Rohit obtained more marks than Tarun, But less than Kabir. Raj obtained more than Vansh, but less then Harshit. Kabir obtained less than Vansh. Who obtained the highest marks?
   (a) Kabir (b) Harshit
   (c) Raj (d) Vansh

3. Mohit is older than Rajesh and Raman. Namit is older than Rajesh, but Younger than Rajeev. Raman is older than Rajeev. Who among them is the oldest?
   (a) Rajeev (b) Rajesh
   (c) Mohit (d) Namit

4. Nimish is 6th from the left end and Avi is 10th from the right end in a row of boys. If there are eight boys between Nimish and Avi then how many boys are there in the row?
   (a) 21 (b) 23
   (c) 24 (d) 25

5. In a row of girls, if Tripti who is 10th from the left and Tusha who is 9th from the right interchange their positions, tripti becomes 15th from the left. How many girls are there in the row?
   (a) 23 (b) 31
   (c) 27 (d) 28

6. Calculate the total number of girls needed to make it 50, if rank of a girl in that group is 7th from the top and 28th from the bottom.
   (a) 15 (b) 16 (c) 17 (d) 18

7. Rank of Sameer is 14th from the top in a group of 25 students. Find his rank from top if 3 new students will be added to the bottom of the list.
   (a) 14 (b) 11 (c) 12 (d) 13

8. In a row of mango trees, one tree is six from either end of the row. How many mango trees are there in the row?
   (a) 10 (b) 11
   (c) 12 (d) 13

9. If Himanshu finds that he is 15th from the right end in a line of boys and fourth from the left end, how many boys should be added to the line such that there are 30 boys in the line?
   (a) 12 (b) 13 (c) 14 (d) 15

10. Shubi ranks 23rd from the top and 36th from the bottom in a class. How many students are there in the class?
    (a) 59 (b) 57 (c) 60 (d) 58

11. In a row of ten boys, when Rohit was shifted by two places towards the left, he became seventh from the left end. What was his earlier position from the right end of the row?
    (a) First (b) Second
    (c) Third (d) Sixth

2 Marks Questions

12. The rank of X is 6th from left and rank of Y is 18th from right hand side in a row of letters. Calculate the extra number of letters required to make it a group of 30, if there are 6 letters present in between X and Y.

(a) 3 (b) 5
(c) 7 (d) No letters

13. Students line up in a queue in which Arham stands 15th from the left and Miransh is 7th from the right. If they interchange their places, Miransh would be 15th from the right.
How many students are there is the queue?

(a) 21 (b) 22
(c) 28 (d) 29

14. In a line of boys facing North, Anni is 19th from the right end and Shubh is 20th from the left end. If there are 6 boys between them and Anni is in the left of Shubh. What is the total number of boys in the line?

(a) 34 (b) 31
(c) 29 (d) 32

15. In a sequence, Gaurav is 10th from the front while Sarthak is 25th from behind and Archie is just in the middle of two. If there are 50 persons in the queue, what position does Archie occupy from the front?

(a) 21th (b) 17th
(c) 18th (d) 13th

16. In a row of girls facing North, Reena is 10th to the left of Pallavi, who is 21st from the right end. If Malini, who is 17th from the left end is fourth to the right of Reena, how many girls are there in a row?

(a) 37 (b) 43
(c) 44 (d) Data Inadequate

17. Five friends P, Q, R, S and T read a newspaper. The one who reads first gives it to R. The one who reads last had taken it from P. T was neither the first nor the last one to read. There were two readers between Q and P. Who reads the newspaper last?

(a) P (b) Q
(c) R (d) S

Chapter 07

Direction Sense Test

There are four main directions i.e., East, West, North and South and four subdirections i.e., North-East, North-West, South-East and South-West.

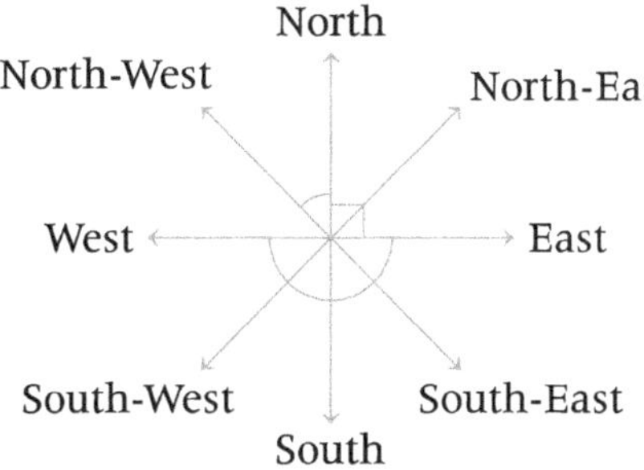

Problem on direction sense test broadly classified into three categories.

Direction Based

This type of questions are based on finding only directions.

EXAMPLE 1 You go North, turn right and then go to left. In which direction are you moving now?

(a) North (b) East (c) South (d) West

Sol. (a)

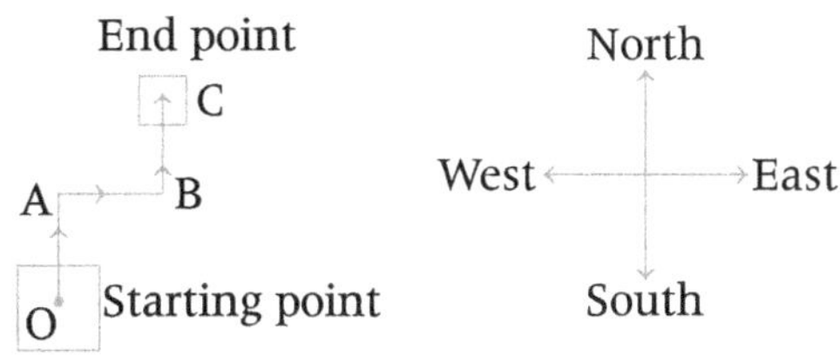

When we compare above diagram with standard direction diagram, we see that the final movement is in the direction BC i.e., North.

Hence, option (a) is correct.

Distance Based

This type of questions are based only on finding the distance.

EXAMPLE 2 Sagar moves 5 km towards East, then turns left, after covering 3 km he turns to left and covers 2 km. Find the total distance covered by Sagar.

(a) 8 km (b) 7 km

(c) 10 km (d) 5 km

Sol. (c)

2 km
C B
3 km
Starting point O
5 km A

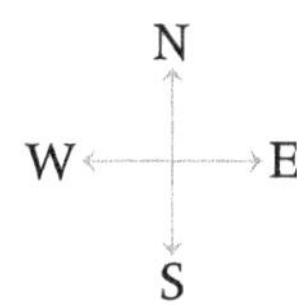

From the above direction graph, total distance covered by Sagar $= OA + AB + BC$

$= 5 + 3 + 2$

$= 10$ km

Hence, option (c) is correct.

Direction and Distance Based

This type of questions are based on finding both direction and distance.

EXAMPLE 3 Prakash walked 50 m toward East, then take a right turn and walked 40 m, again take a right turn and walked 50 m. How far and in which direction is he from his initial position?

(a) 20 m, East
(b) 40m, West
(c) 90 m, North
(d) 40 m, South

Sol. (d) According to the question,

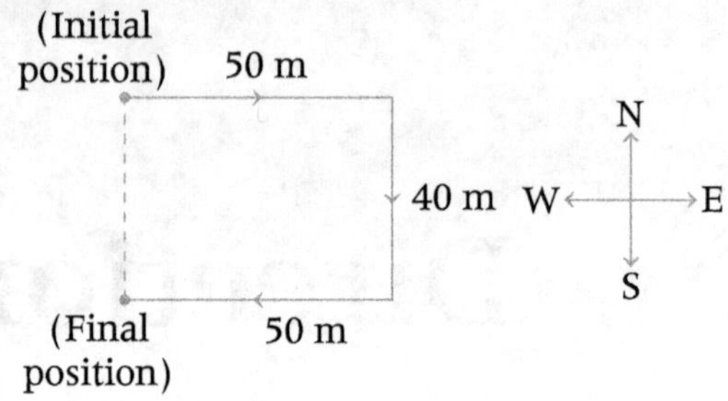

Prakash is 40 m away and in South direction from his initial point.
Hence option (d) is correct.

Let's Practice

1 Mark Questions

1. Seema started walking towards South. She took a right turn after walking 5 m. She again took a left turn after walking 2 m. In which direction is she facing now?
   (a) South (b) East
   (c) North (d) West

2. If 'South-East' is called 'South', 'North-West' is called 'North', 'South-West' is called 'West', and so on, what will 'East' be called?
   (a) East
   (b) North-East
   (c) South-East
   (d) North

3. A is South-West of B, C is the South-East of B, then C is in which direction of A?
   (a) West (b) East
   (c) South (d) North-East

4. Kavita was facing bus stop (in south) at the beginning. She turned clockwise to face East. What angle did she turn through?

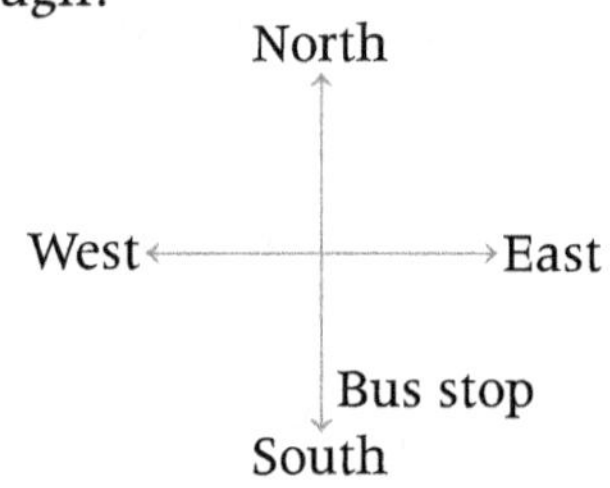

   (a) 90° (b) 180°
   (c) 270° (d) 360°

5. A boy first goes in South direction, then he turns torwards left and travels for some distance. After that he turns right and moves certain distance. At last he turns left and travels again for some distance. Now, in which direction is he moving?
   (a) South (b) West
   (c) East (d) North

6. Kamal is facing towards North and turns through 45° anti-clockwise, then 135° clockwise and again 90° clockwise. In which direction is he facing now?
(a) East (b) West
(c) North (d) South

7. A ship is sailing towards South-East. The captain ordered to turn the ship by angle of 135° in anti-clockwise direction and then 225° in clockwise direction. In which direction is it sailing now?
(a) North-West (b) South
(c) South-West (d) East

8. Ashwini goes 8 km towards East, then he goes 4 km towards South. In the end, he goes 4 km towards East. Find the total distance covered by Ashwini.
(a) 8 km (b) 16 km (c) 20 km (d) 10 km

9. Shravan goes Northward 10 m. He turns left and walks 30 m, then he again turns left and walks 50 m, then how much distance Shravan travelled?
(a) 60 m (b) 20 m (c) 10 m (d) 90 m

10. A man walked 3 km towards North, then 8 km towards South. His position at the end of the walk is
(a) 5 km towards East
(b) 3 km towards South
(c) 8 km towards North
(d) 5 km towards South

2 Marks Questions

11. Vikas is facing towards West and turns through 90° clockwise, again 45° clockwise and then turns through 180° anti-clockwise. In which direction is he facing now?
(a) North-West
(b) South-West
(c) North-East
(d) South

12. One morning, Ram started to walk towards the Sun. After covering some distance he turned to the left, then again to the right and after covering some distance he again turn to the left. Now, in which direction is he facing?
(a) North-East (b) East
(c) North (d) West

13. From her home Suhani walked 40 m towards South. She turned left and walked 50 m. Then she turned left and walked 40 m. She again turned left and walked 60 m and reached school. How far is school from Suhani's home?
(a) 15 m
(b) 5 m
(c) 10 m
(d) 20 m

14. Point R is 20 m North of point B. Point J is exactly in the middle of the points R and B. Point N is 7m East of point B. Point M is 7m East of point J. Point S is 13 m North of point M. What is the distance between S and N and S is in which direction with respect to J?
(a) 23 m, North-East
(b) 25m, North
(c) 25 m, South
(d) 23 m, North-West

Blood Relations

Mainly there are two types of blood relations

Relations on mother's side are called **maternal relations**.

Relations on father's side are called **paternal relations**.

EXAMPLE 1. Vimal is the brother of Renu. Renu is the mother of Kunal. How is Kunal related to Vimal?

(a) Uncle (b) Father
(c) Nephew (d) Son

Sol. (c) Renu is the sister of Vimal and Kunal is the son of Renu. So, Kunal is the son of Vimal's sister i.e., nephew. The relation diagram can be drawn as :

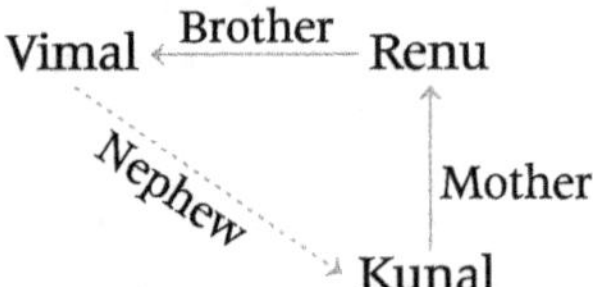

Hence, option (c) is correct.

EXAMPLE 2. Pointing to a lady, I said, 'She is the mother of my father's sister'. How is that lady related to me?

(a) Grandmother (b) Mother
(c) Daughter (d) Granddaughter

Sol. (a) My father's sister is my aunt and my aunt's mother is also my father's mother. So, she is my grandmother.

The relation diagram can be represented as

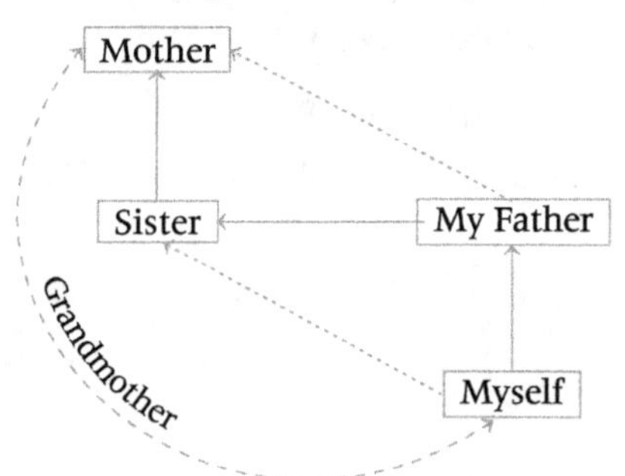

Hence, option (a) is correct.

EXAMPLE 3. P and Q are sisters. A and B are brothers. P's daughter is A's sister. How is Q related to B?

(a) Aunt
(b) Uncle
(c) Mother
(d) Grandmother

Sol. (a) P's daughter is A's sister and A and B are brothers.

So, P is the mother of A and B. Q is the sister of B's mother, so she is his aunt.

The relation diagram can be drawn as

P ←Sisters→ Q ← Aunt ... B

Daughter ←Sister→ A ←Brother→ B

Hence, option (a) is correct.

So, P is the mother of A and B. Q is the sister of B's mother, so she is his aunt.

The relation diagram can be drawn as

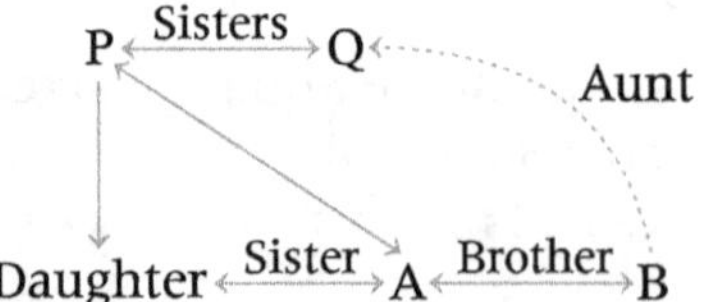

Hence, option (a) is correct.

Let's Practice

1 Mark Questions

1. I am brother of Sunil and Meena, Mr. Rakesh is my father's father. How is Meena related to Mr. Rakesh?
   (a) Daughter
   (b) Sister
   (c) Granddaughter
   (d) Mother

2. Ramu is my father's real brother. Janvi is my grandmother. How is Ramu related to Janvi?
   (a) Brother (b) Father
   (c) Uncle (d) Son

3. Seema is the daughter of Radhika. Mohan is the brother of Radhika. Kirti is the wife of Mohan. How is Kirti related to Seema?
   (a) Sister (b) Aunt
   (c) Mother (d) Grandmother

4. If A is the sister of B and B is the brother of C. C is the father of D, then how is A related to D?
   (a) Mother (b) Sister
   (c) Sister-in-law (d) Aunt

5. Pointing to a man in photograph, Radhika says, "His father's daughter is my sister". How is Radhika related to that man?
   (a) Daughter (b) Sister
   (c) Mother (d) Sister-in-law

6. Kunal says, "Ayushi's mother is the only daughter of my mother-in-law". How is Ayushi related to Kunal?
   (a) Wife (b) Mother
   (c) Aunt (d) Daughter

7. A boy introduced a woman as the only daughter of the father of his mother. How is boy related to woman?
   (a) Brother (b) Father
   (c) Uncle (d) Son

8. A man said to Vimal, "Your mother's husband is my brother-in-law". How is man related to Vimal?
   (a) Uncle (b) Father
   (c) Father-in-law (d) Brother

9. Pointing to a woman, Karan said, "She is the sister of my son's mother". How is woman related to Karan?
   (a) Sister (b) Mother
   (c) Sister-in-law (d) Aunt

10. P and Q are sisters. A and B are brothers. P's daughter is A's sister. How is Q related to B?
    (a) Aunt
    (b) Uncle
    (c) Mother
    (d) Grandmother

2 Marks Questions

11. A and B are brothers. C and D are brothers and C's mother is A's wife. How is D related to B?

    (a) Niece
    (b) Nephew
    (c) Uncle
    (d) Son

12. Aditya is Bhavi's brother. Bharat is Jayant's father. Esha is Bhavi's mother. Aditya and Jayant are brothers. What is Esha's relationship with Bharat?

    (a) Sister
    (b) Mother
    (c) Daughter
    (d) Wife

13. Ritesh is son of Varun. Sarika, Varun's sister has a son Rahul and a daughter Riya. Sahil is the maternal uncle of Rahul. How is Ritesh related to Rahul?

    (a) Nephew (b) Cousin
    (c) Uncle (d) Father

Directions (Q. Nos. 14-17) Study the following information carefully and answer the questions that follow.
Members of a family A, B, C, D, E, F and G are sitting together. A is son of G who is brother of F. F is mother of E and B.
E is brother of B and B is sister of C. C is a male. D is a female and child of C.

14. How is B related to A?

    (a) Cousin (b) Mother
    (c) Aunt (d) Sister-in-law

15. Which of the following is the pair of female?

    (a) BA (b) GF (c) FC (d) FB

16. How many male members are there in the family?

    (a) 1 (b) 2
    (c) 3 (d) 4

17. Who is the uncle of C?

    (a) E (b) A
    (c) G (d) D

Puzzles

'Puzzle' is a problem in which the information is given in a confusing or jumbled manner. Many a times, only a part of the whole information is given and the students are required to find the missing links in the given information and answer the questions. In puzzle test, following types of questions are generally asked.

EXAMPLE 1 Read the following information carefully and answer the questions given below.

Six friends A, B, C, D, E and F are sitting in a circle facing the centre. A is sitting between B and E. C is sitting between D and F. E is sitting to the immediate right of D.

(i) Who is sitting between E and C?
(a) D (b) B (c) A (d) F

(ii) Who is sitting immediate right of A?
(a) B (b) D (c) E (d) C

Sol. A is sitting between B and E. Since, the positions of B and E are not clear, so the possible diagram will be

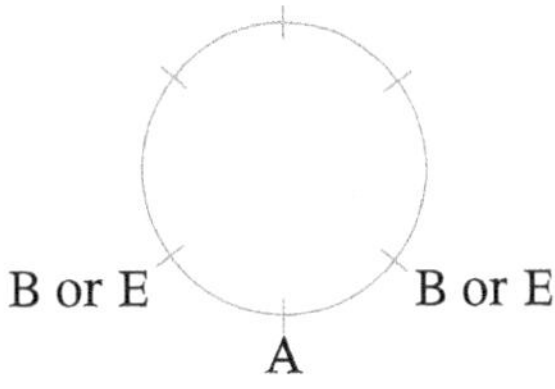

C is sitting between D and F.

Here, again the positions of D and F are not clear, so the possible diagram will be

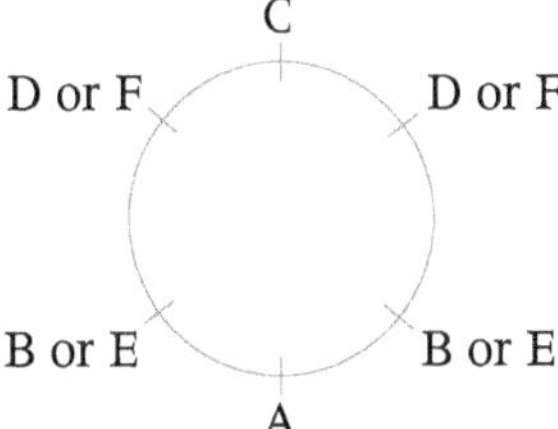

Now, E is to the immediate right of D.

Then,

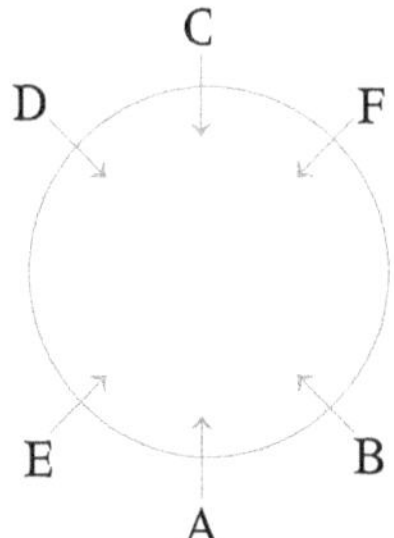

(i) (a) As shown in the above diagram D, is between E and C.
Hence, option (a) is correct.

(ii) (a) As shown in the above diagram, B is immediate rightof A.
Hence, option (a) is correct.

Let's Practice

1 Mark Questions

Directions (Q. Nos. 1 and 2) Read the following information carefully to answer the questions given below:

(i) Kailash, Govind and Harinder are intelligent.

(ii) Kailash, Rajesh and Jitendra are hard-working.

(iii) Rajesh, Harinder and Jitendra are honest.

(iv) Kailash, Govind and Jitendra are ambitious.

1. Which of the following persons is neither hard-working nor ambitious?

(a) Kailash (b) Govind
(c) Harinder (d) Rajesh

2. Which of the following persons is neither honest nor hard-working but is ambitious?

(a) Kailash (b) Govind
(c) Harinder (d) Rajesh

Directions (Q.Nos. 3-5) Read the following information and answer the questions given below.

Five girls are sitting on a bench to be photographed.

(i) Seema is to the left of Rani and to the right of Bindu.

(ii) Garima is to right of Rani.

(iii) Reeta is between Rani and Garima.

3. Who is in the middle of the photograph?

(a) Bindu (b) Rani
(c) Reeta (d) Seema

4. Who is second from the left in photograph?

(a) Reeta (b) Garima
(c) Bindu (d) Seema

5. Who is second from the right?

(a) Garima (b) Rani
(c) Reeta (d) Bindu

Directions (Q. Nos. 6 and 7) Read the following information and answer the questions given below.

A, B, C, D, E and F are sitting along a circle facing at the centre and are playing cards.

(i) E is the neighbour of A and D.

(ii) F is on the immediate right of A.

(iii) B is not the neighbour of D.

6. Who are the neighbours of B?

(a) C and D (b) F and C
(c) A and E (d) F and D

7. What is the position of F from E?

(a) Immediate Left
(b) Third to the right of E
(c) Second to the right of E
(d) Immediate right

Directions (Q. Nos. 8-10) Read the following information carefully and answers the questions given below it.

(i) A, B, C, M, N, O, X and Y are sitting round the circle and facing the centre.

(ii) A is second to the right of N who is the neighbour of C and X.

(iii) M is not the neighbour of A.

(iv) X is the neighbour of O.

(v) B is not between M and Y. Y is not between O and M.

8. What is the position of M?

(a) Between O and Y
(b) Second to the right of A
(c) To the immediate right of A
(d) Data inadequate

9. Which two of the following are not neighbours?
   (a) C and X (b) O and X
   (c) C and A (d) B and Y

10. Which of the following is correct?
   (a) C is between O and X.
   (b) O is between Y and M.
   (c) B is to the immediate left of Y.
   (d) A is to the immediate right of B.

Directions (Q. Nos. 11-13) Study the information carefully to answer the questions given below:

There are 6 painters A, P, R, X, S and M are sitting in a row. S and M are in the middle of the row. A and P are at the ends of the row. R is sitting to the left of A.

11. Who is sitting immediate right of P ?
   (a) P (b) X (c) M (d) S

12. Which of the following position 'A' is sitting?
   (a) First from right end
   (b) First from left end
   (c) Second to the right end
   (d) Third from the left end

13. Which two of the following are immediate neighbours?
   (a) RS (b) AM (c) XS (d) XA

2 Marks Questions

Directions (Q. Nos. 14-16) Study the information carefully, to answer the questions given below.
In a school, there were five teachers A, B, C, D and E. A and B were teaching Hindi and English. C and B were teaching English and Geography. D and A were teaching Mathematics and Hindi. E and B were teaching History and French.

14. Who among the following teachers was teaching maximum number of subjects?
   (a) A (b) B (c) C (d) D

15. More than two teachers are teaching which common subjects?
   (a) History (b) Hindi
   (c) English (d) Both (b) and (c)

16. D, B and A were teaching which of the following subjects?
   (a) English only
   (b) Hindi and English
   (c) Hindi only
   (d) English and Geography

17. Five students are standing in a row facing East. Maya is to the left of Suraj, Tiya and Samsul. Suraj, Tiya and Samsul are to the left of Ankit. Samsul is between Suraj and Tiya. If Tiya is fourth from the left, then what is the position of Suraj from the right end?
   (a) Second (b) First
   (c) Third (d) Fourth

Chapter 10

Mathematical Reasoning

'Mathematical Reasoning' is all about playing with numbers. Problems based on this chapter test a student's ability to figure out the rule (or pattern), which exists in a given arrangement of numbers, letters or combination of letters and numbers. Problems based on mathematical reasoning can be broadly classified into the following four categories

- VBODMAS Operation
- Symbolic Operation
- Statement Based
- Unitary Method Based

VBODMAS Operation

There are four fundamental operations. These are addition (+), Subtraction (−), Multiplication (×) and division (÷).

Whenever, two or more these operations occur simultaneously, we solve such complex problems by applying the 'VBODMAS' rule. Let us explain this rule briefly.

Do first	V	Vinculum	$\overline{AB}$
	B	Brackets	( ), [ ], { }
	O	Power Of	$\sqrt{}$, $(\ )^2$
	D	Division	/, ÷
	M	Multiplication	×
	A	Addition	+
Do last	S	Subtraction	−

EXAMPLE 1 If '+' means '÷', '−' means '×', '×' means '+' and '÷' means '−', then what is the value of

$$45 \div 40 + 8 \times 20 - 2 \ ?$$

(a) 100 (b) 80
(c) 120 (d) 90

Sol. (b) On substituting the signs as given in the question, we get

Expression $= 45 - 40 \div 8 + 20 \times 2$

Simplify the above expression using VBODMAS rule,

$45 - 40 \div 8 + 20 \times 2$

$= 45 - 5 + 20 \times 2$ [division, $40 \div 8 = 5$]

$= 45 - 5 + 40$ [multiplication, $20 \times 2 = 40$]

[addition, $45 + 40 = 85$]

$= 85 - 5$

$= 80$ [subtraction, $85 - 5 = 80$]

Hence, option (b) is correct.

Symbolic Operation

Problems based on 'Symbolic Operation' involve simplification of a given arithmetic expression.

In such type of operation, the mathematical operators like addition (+), subtraction (−), multiplication (×) and division (÷) are represented by symbols and students are required to substitute the symbols with actual operations to get the answer.

EXAMPLE 2 If '<' stands for '+', '>' stands for '–', '@' stands for '×' and '#' stands for '÷', then, find the value of

160 > 10@ (140 # 5 > 14).

(a) 34 (b) 40
(c) 48 (d) 20

Sol. (d) We have, 160 > 10@ (140 # 5 > 14)

On substituting the signs we get,

$$160 - 10 \times (140 \div 5 - 14)$$

Simplify the above expression using VBODMAS rule

$$160 - 10 \times (140 \div 5 - 14)$$
$$= 160 - 10 \times (28 - 14)$$
$$= 160 - 10 \times (14) = 160 - 140 = 20$$

Hence, option (d) is correct.

Unitary Method Based

In simple terms, the unitary method is used to find the value of a single unit from a given multiple.

EXAMPLE 3 If the cost of 15 bananas is ₹ 90, then find the cost of 3 dozen bananas?

(a) ₹ 36 (b) ₹ 136 (c) ₹ 216 (d) ₹ 160

Sol. (c) Given, Cost of 15 bananas = ₹ 90

Cost of 1 banana $= \frac{90}{15} =$ ₹ 6

∴ Cost of 3 dozen $(3 \times 12 = 36)$ bananas

$= 36 \times 6 =$ ₹216

Hence, option (c) is correct.

Let's Practice

1 Mark Questions

Directions (Q. Nos. 1and 2) Read the information carefully and answer the questions given below:

If '+' means '×', '–' means '÷', '×' means '–' and '÷' means '+', then find the value of the given expressions.

1. $24 + 2 \times 4 \div 6 - 3$

(a) 50 (b) 46
(c) 48 (d) 52

2. $5 \times 4 \div 6 + 5 - 4$

(a) – 6.5 (b) – 5.5
(c) 8.5 (d) 6

3. If '+' denotes 'multiplication', '×' denotes 'subtraction', '÷' denotes 'addition' and '–' denotes 'division', then $350 - 50 \div 10 + 40 \times 6 + 20 = ?$

(a) 185 (b) 287
(c) 200 (d) 191

4. If $2 * 3 = 8, 3 * 2 = 9$ and $5 * 1 = 5$, then find the value of $4 * 3$.

(a) 72 (b) 64
(c) 78 (d) 80

5. If 6 ★5 = 31, 7★8 = 57, 3★4 = 13, 9★ 10 = ?

(a) 90 (b) 91
(c) 81 (d) 19

6. If $P = 8, Q = 5, R = 14$ and $S = 7$, then $P \times Q + R \div S = ?$

(a) 24 (b) 38
(c) 42 (d) 84

7. If '@' stands for 'add', '#' stands for 'subtract','%' stands for 'divide' and '&' stands for 'multiply' then what is the value of (9 & 3) # 12@ 10?

(a) 23 (b) 20 (c) 17 (d) 25

8. Which of the following set of signs should be used to replace symbol '@' in the following?

$$25@2@6 = 4@11@0$$

(a) $\times, -, \times, +$ (b) $+, -, \times, +$
(c) $\times, +, \times, -$ (d) $\times, +, +, \times$

9. Which of the following interchanges of signs and numbers will make the equation correct?

$$4 + 5 \times 2 = 13$$

(a) $\times$ and $+$, 5 and 2
(b) $+$ and $\times$, 4 and 2
(c) $+$ and $\times$, 4 and 5
(d) None of the above

10. In the following question, by using which mathematical operators will the expression become correct ?

15 ...... 3 ...... 8 40

(a) $\times, \div$ and $>$ (b) $\div, \times$ and $<$
(c) $\div, \times$ and $=$ (d) $+, \times$ and $=$

11. Which of the following signs, if changed, will make the equation correct?

$$50 \times 5 \div 4 + 4 = 44$$

(a) $\div$ and $\times$ (b) $\div$ and $+$
(c) $\times$ and $+$ (d) None of these

12. Mohan can walk 121 km in 11 h. What distance can he walk in 6 h?
(a) 96 km (b) 66 km (c) 76 km (d) 56 km

13. In a hostel, 240 students consume 1440 kg of rice per month. How much rice will be consumed by 150 students in a month?
(a) 8001 kg (b) 7050 kg
(c) 900 kg (d) 1575 kg

14. The cost of 90 L of petrol is ₹ 5400. How much will 18 L of petrol cost?
(a) ₹ 1200 (b) ₹ 1080
(c) ₹ 1409 (d) ₹ 2020

2 Marks Questions

15. If '+' stands for '×', '×' stands for '–', '–' stands for '÷' and '÷' stands for '+', then

$$(32 \div 128 - 16 \times 8 + 4) - (4 + 30 \div 30 - 6 \times 16) = ?$$

(a) 109/8 (b) 111/9 (c) 8/109 (d) 9/127

16. If in a certain symbolic form
P $ Q, means divide
P # Q, means subtract
P % Q, means add
P @ Q, means multiply
then, 35#15%40$10@5 = ?
(a) 30 (b) 40 (c) 10 (d) 5

17. If $\uparrow$ means '+', $\downarrow$ means '–', $\leftarrow$ means '×' and $\rightarrow$ means '÷', then what is the value of $1 \uparrow 41 \leftarrow 5 \uparrow 37 \downarrow 91 \rightarrow 7$?
(a) 225 (b) 228
(c) 230 (d) 242

18. The annual rent of Mr. Gupta's house is ₹ 3600. Find the rent of 5 months?
(a) ₹ 1690
(b) ₹ 1785
(c) ₹ 1500
(d) ₹ 1800

Inserting the Missing Characters

A pattern is a design or a set of figures and it contains numbers or letters or both. Each of these has some characters. Out of these characters a number/letter is missing.

To identify the missing number/letter candidate need to crack the reasoning or logic behind this pattern so as to find the missing term.

In 'Inserting the Missing Characters' following types of questions are generally asked.

EXAMPLE 1 Which number will replace the question mark(?)?

$\frac{1}{2}$	$\frac{1}{4}$	$\frac{1}{4}$
$\frac{1}{3}$	$\frac{1}{6}$	$\frac{1}{6}$
$\frac{1}{2}$	$\frac{1}{3}$	?

(a) $\frac{1}{2}$ (b) $\frac{1}{6}$ (c) $\frac{1}{9}$ (d) $\frac{5}{6}$

Sol. (b) Here, in I row, $\frac{1}{2}-\frac{1}{4}=\frac{1}{4}$

and in II row, $\frac{1}{3}-\frac{1}{6}=\frac{1}{6}$

Similarly, in III row, $\frac{1}{2}-\frac{1}{3}=\boxed{\frac{1}{6}}$

Hence, option (b) is correct.

EXAMPLE 2 Which one of the given options will replace the question mark (?)?

K	L	M
O	P	Q
T	U	?

(a) Z (b) V (c) A (d) W

Sol. (b) Considering rowwise,

In I row, $K \xrightarrow{+1} L \xrightarrow{+1} M$,

In II row, $O \xrightarrow{+1} P \xrightarrow{+1} Q$

Similarly, in III, row, $T \xrightarrow{+1} U \xrightarrow{+1} \boxed{V}$

Hence, option (b) is correct.

EXAMPLE 3 Which letter will replace the question mark(?)?

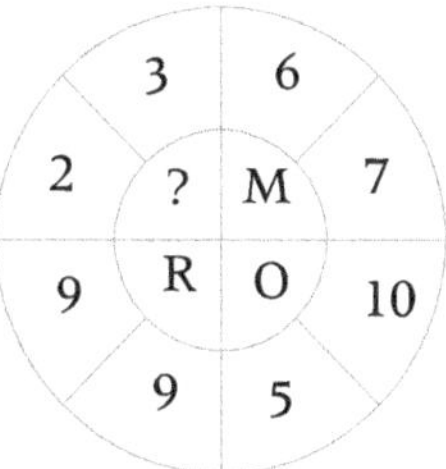

(a) Y (b) U (c) I (d) E

Sol. (d) As, $6+7=13 \rightarrow M, 10+5=15 \rightarrow O$ and $9+9=18 \rightarrow R$.

Similarly, $2+3=5 \rightarrow \boxed{E}$

Hence, option (d) is correct.

Let's Practice

1 Mark Questions

1. Which number will replace the question mark(?)?

6	7	8
10	16	22
8	?	6

(a) 7 (b) 10 (c) 14 (d) 12

2. Find the missing number.

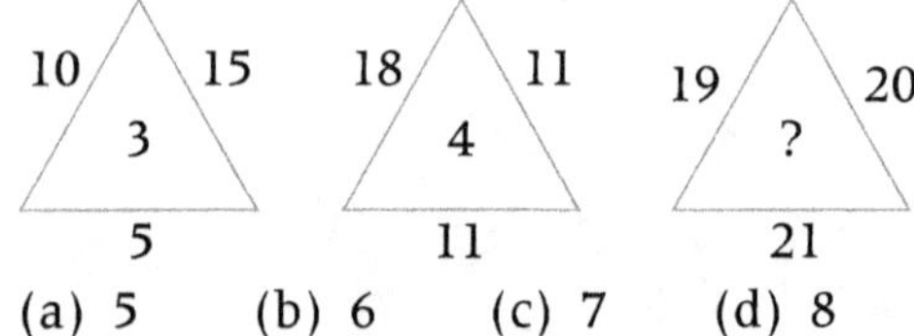

(a) 5 (b) 6 (c) 7 (d) 8

3. Which number will replace the question mark(?)?

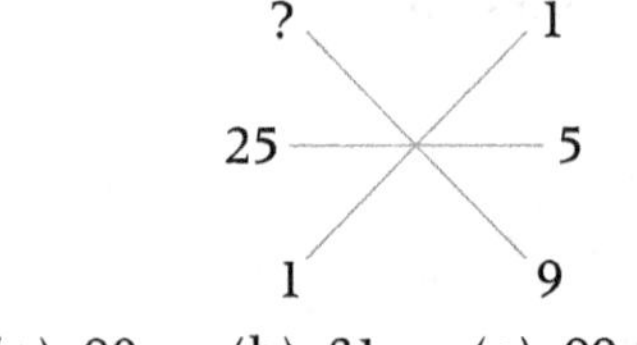

(a) 90 (b) 81 (c) 99 (d) 29

4. Which number will replace the question mark(?)?

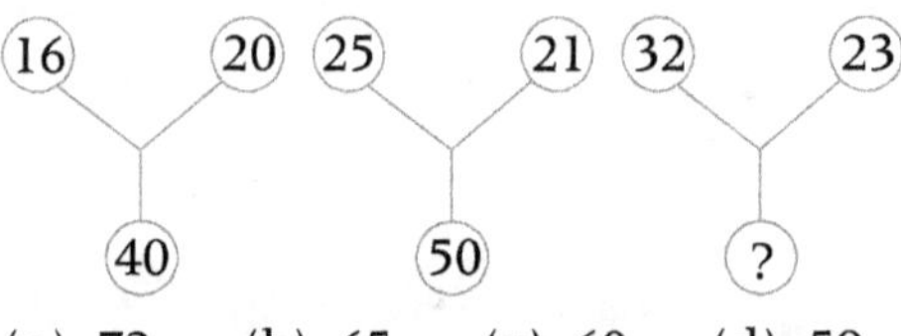

(a) 72 (b) 65 (c) 60 (d) 59

5. Find the missing number.

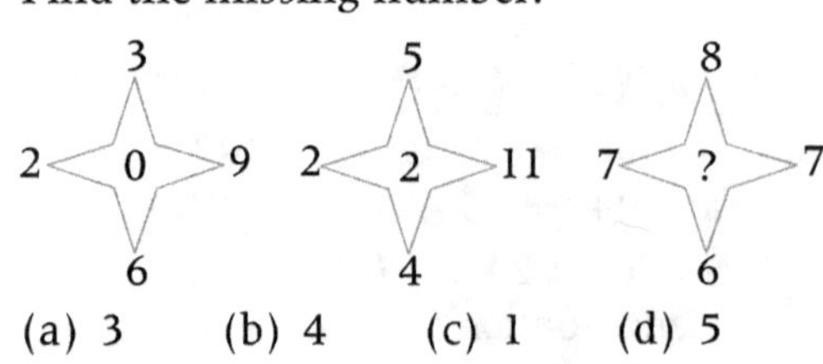

(a) 3 (b) 4 (c) 1 (d) 5

6. Find the missing letter.

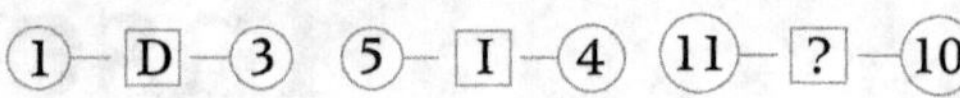

(a) L (b) M
(c) T (d) U

7. Which number will replace the question mark(?)?

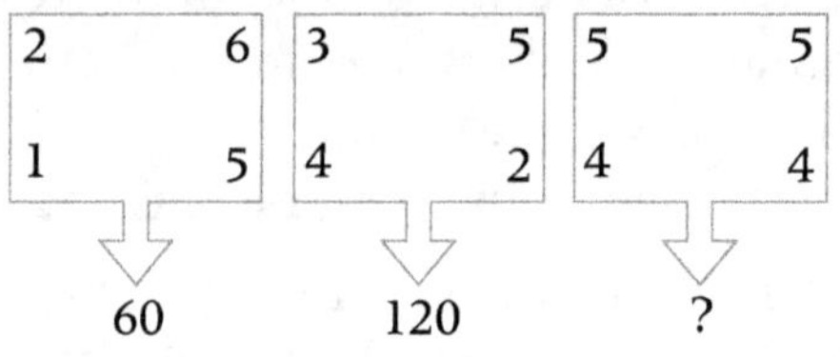

(a) 240 (b) 400
(c) 360 (d) 380

8. Based on the following figure, answer the question given below.

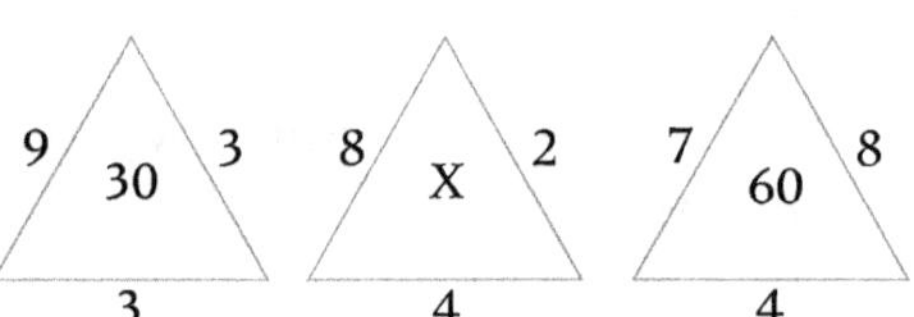

The value of $(X^2 - 1)$ is

(a) 195 (b) 399
(c) 999 (d) 933

9. Find the missing number.

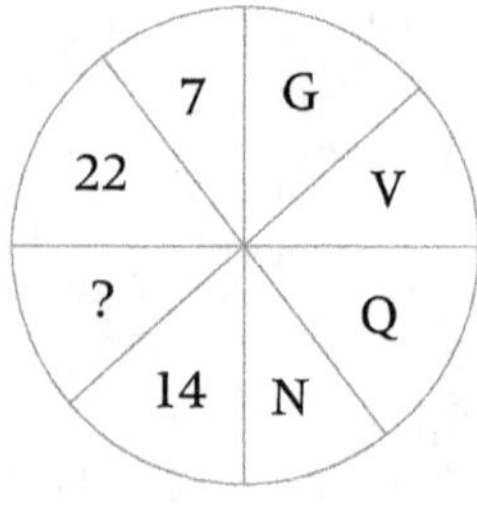

(a) 12 (b) 17 (c) 14 (d) 15

10. Find the number that will replace the question mark(?).

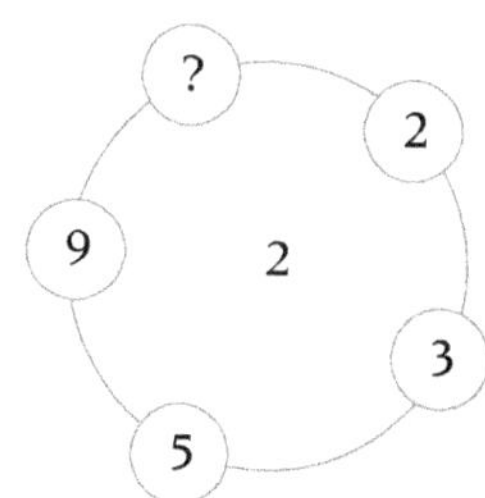

(a) 79 (b) 17
(c) 15 (d) 18

11. Which number will replace the question mark(?)?

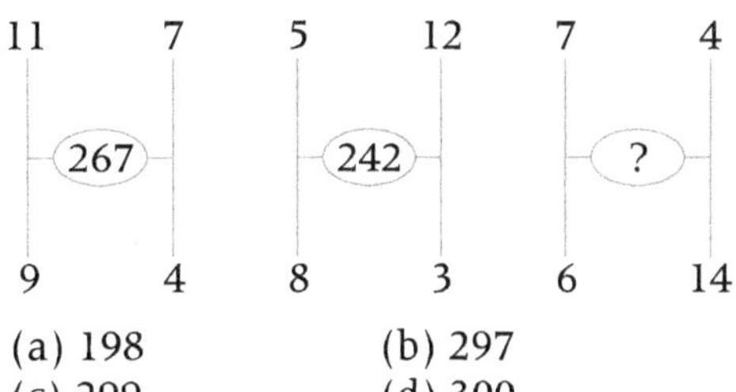

(a) 198 (b) 297
(c) 299 (d) 300

12. Find the missing number.

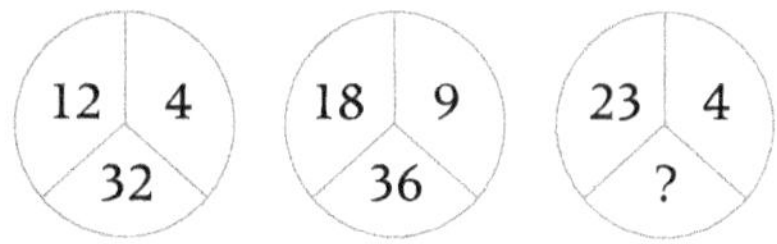

(a) 120 (b) 122 (c) 118 (d) 125

13. Which number will replace the question mark (?)?

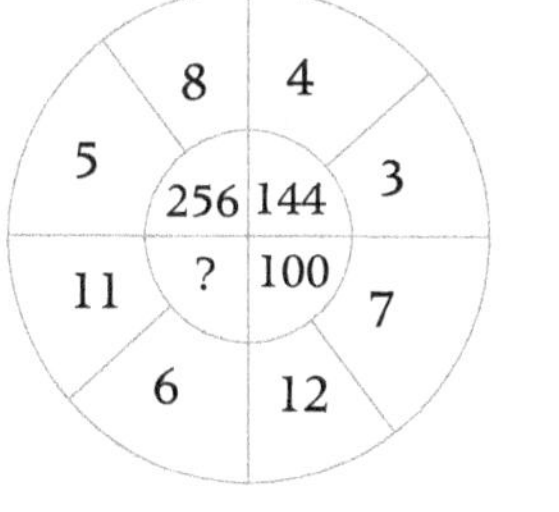

(a) 86 (b) 56 (c) 66 (d) 76

14. Find the missing number.

8 4
5 3
256 144
? 100
11 7
6 12

(a) 324 (b) 576 (c) 343 (d) 164

2 Marks Questions

15. Which number will replace the question mark(?)?

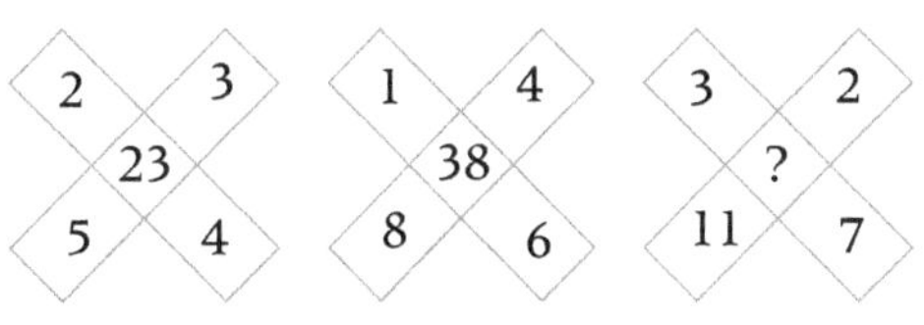

(a) 43 (b) 42 (c) 44 (d) 41

16. Find the missing letter.

A	G	M
C	I	?
E	K	Q

(a) O (b) N (c) P (d) R

17. Complete the following matrix.

Z_2	X_{19}	V_{66}
A_3	C_{20}	?
T_4	R_{21}	P_{68}

(a) E_6 (b) F_{69} (c) W_{67} (d) E_{56}

18. Which number will replace the question mark (?) ?

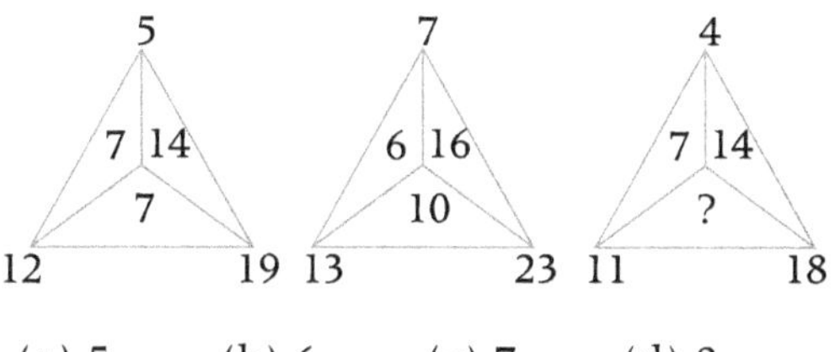

(a) 5 (b) 6 (c) 7 (d) 8

Chapter 12

Mirror Images

The image of an object as seen in a plane mirror is known as mirror image of that object or mirror reflection. In mirror image, the right side of the object appears on the left side and the left side of the object appears on the right side.

Problem based on the mirror image can be classified into three catagories:

Figure Based

In this type, questions are based on finding mirror image of the figures.

EXAMPLE 1

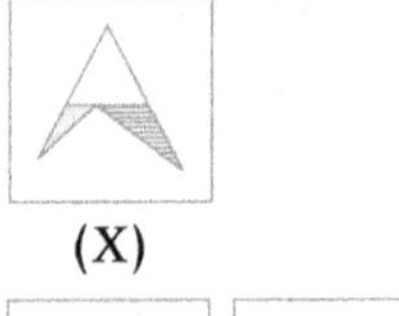

(X)

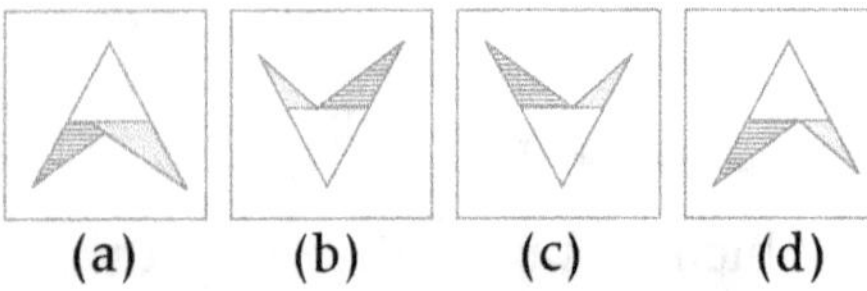

(a) (b) (c) (d)

Sol. (d) The mirror image of the given object is as shown below:

Hence, option (d) correct.

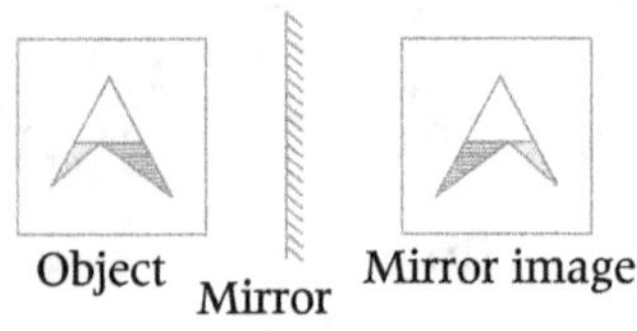

Alphabet Based

In this type, questions are based on finding mirror or image of the alphabets.

EXAMPLE 2. Choose the correct mirror image of the word DISPLAY from the options given below.

(a) ᗡISP⅃AY

(b) ᗡIƧꟼ⅃AY

(c) ᗡIƧPLAY

(d) ᗡISꟼLAY

Sol. (b) The corrrect mirror image of the word is as shown below:

Hence, option (b) is correct.

D	ᗡ
I	I
S	Ƨ
P	ꟼ
L	⅃
A	A
Y	Y

Number Based

In this type questions are based only on mirror images of numbers.

EXAMPLE 3 Choose the correct mirror image?

93184

(a) ߂I3ɘ8 (b) ߂8IƐɘ

(c) 48IƐ9 (d) ߂8IƐɘ

Sol. (d) The correct mirror image is as shown below

93184 | ߂8IƐɘ

Mirror

Hence, option (d) is correct.

Let's Practice

1 Mark Questions

Direction (Q. Nos. 1 and 2) Choose the correct mirror image of the given figure (X), (if mirror is placed vertically right to the figure).

1\.
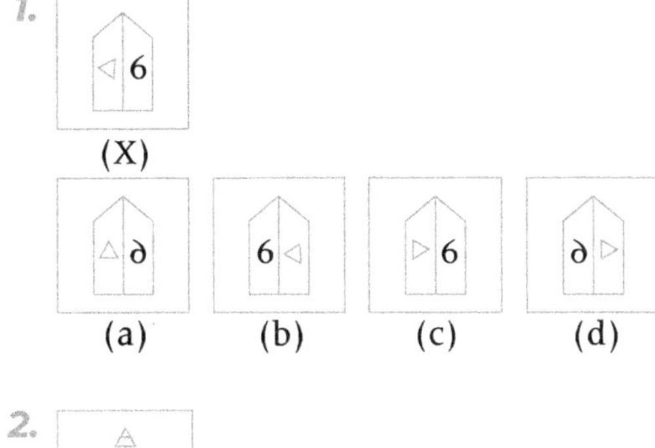

2\.
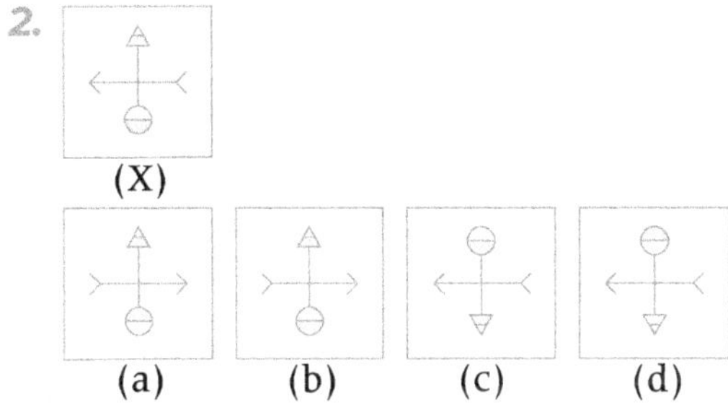

Directions (Q. Nos. 4-8) In each of the following questions, choose the correct mirror image of the given figure (X) (if mirror is placed on vertically left side of the figure).

3\.
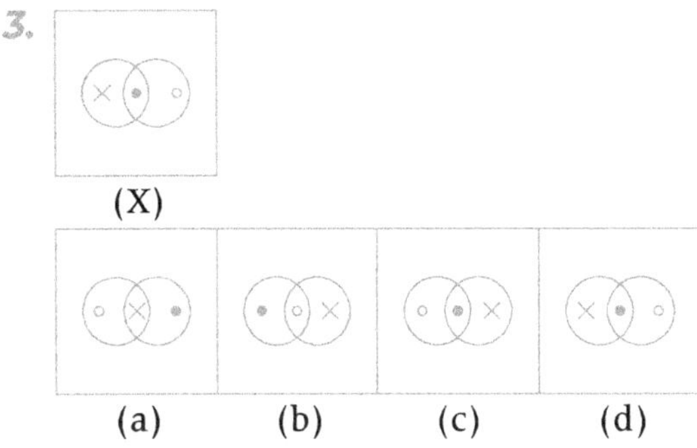

4\.
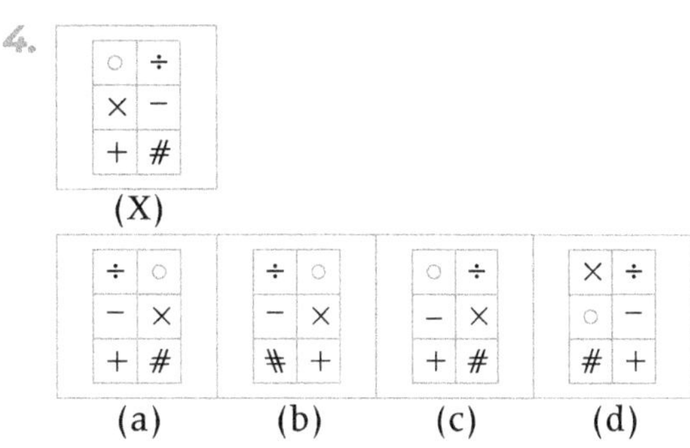

5\.
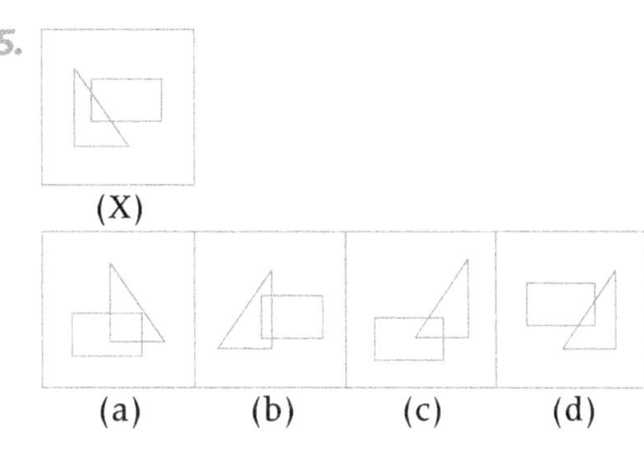

6\.
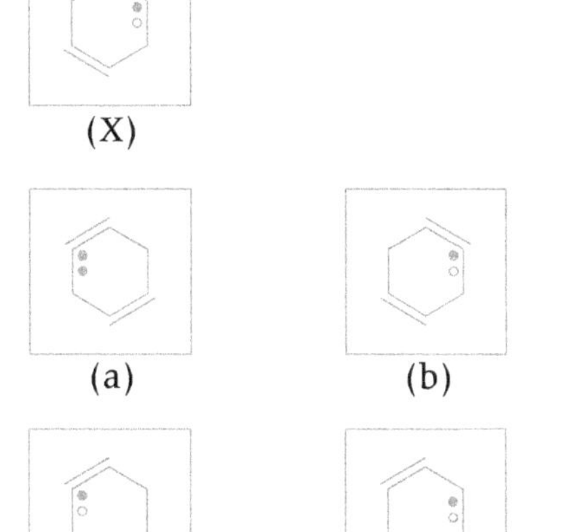

7. Identify the mirror image of the given figure given below.

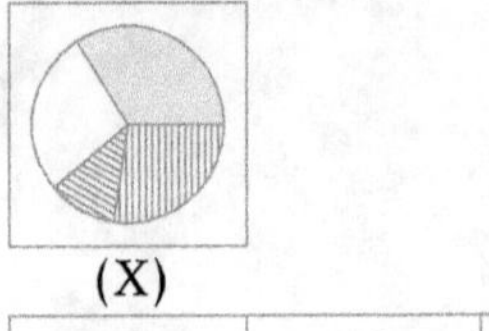

(X)

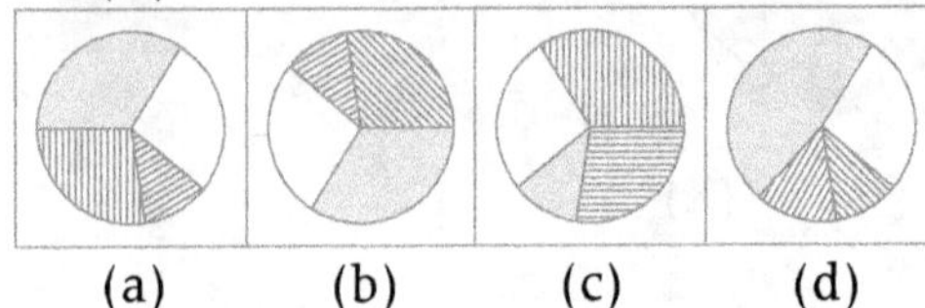

(a) (b) (c) (d)

8. Choose the correct mirror image of the figure given.

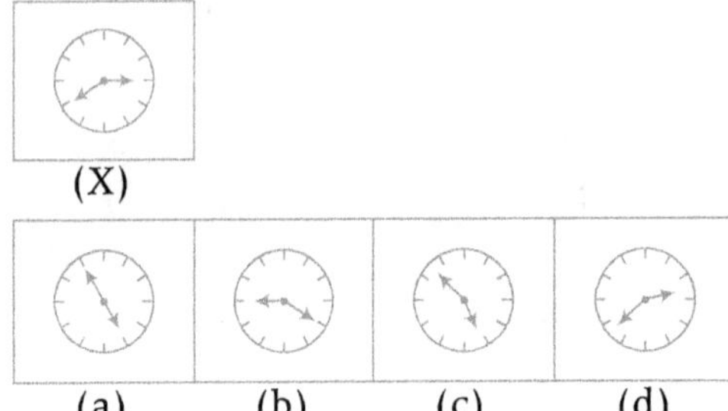

(X)

(a) (b) (c) (d)

Directions (Q. Nos. 9-11) Choose the correct mirror image of the following letters.

9. DI4C

(a) Ɔ4JD (b) Ɔ4JD
(c) Ɔ4Iᗡ (d) Ɔ4Lᗡ

10. TRAIN

(a) ИIAЯT (b) ИIART
(c) NIAЯT (d) ИIATR

11. F U N S T I C K

(a) ꓘƆITSИUF (b) ꓘƆITƧИUꟻ
(c) ꓘƆIƧ И UF (d) KCITƧNUꟻ

Directions (Q.Nos. 12 and 13)
Find the mirror image of the following.

12. 9 6 5 8 3 2

(a) 2 Ɛ 8 5 ∂ 9 (b) Ƨ 3 8 ट ∂ 9
(c) Ƨ 3 8 5 ∂ 9 (d) Ƨ Ɛ 8 ट ∂ ၉

13. C 2 D 8

(a) 8 ᗡ Ƨ Ɔ (c) 8 ᗡ Ƨ C
(b) 8 D Ƨ D (d) D 8 Ƨ ᗡ

2 Marks Questions

14. Identify the mirror image of th given figure.

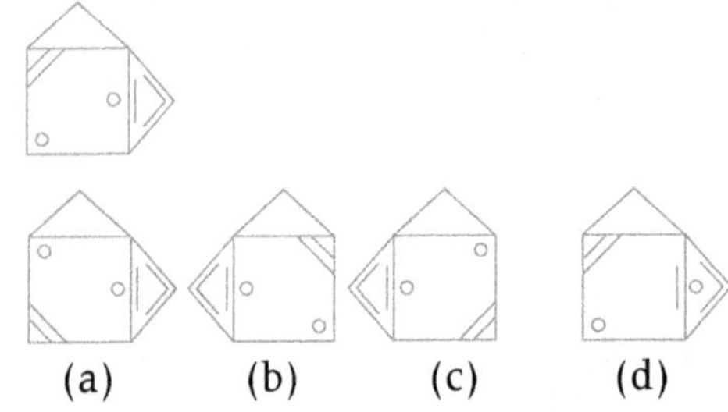

(a) (b) (c) (d)

15. Choose the correct mirror image.

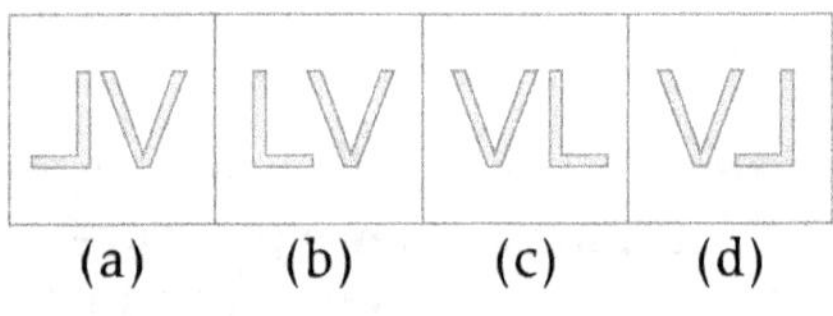

(a) (b) (c) (d)

16. Identify the mirror image of the given figure.

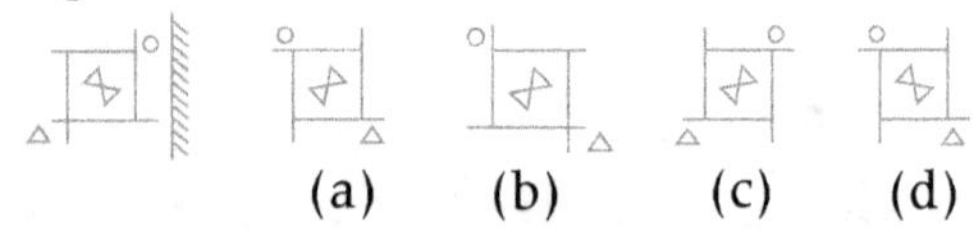

(a) (b) (c) (d)

17. Find the correct miror image of the given set?

59g#t7m%

(a) S%mꓶt#g၉ट (b) %mꓶt#g၉ट
(c) %mꓶt#g၉ट (d) %m7t#g၉ट

Water Images

The reflection of an object as seen in water is known as water image. It is obtained by inverting an object vertically i.e., the upper part of the object will become the lower part and *vice-versa*.

Problems based on the water image can be classified into three categories.

- Figure Based
- Alphabet Based
- Number Based

In this type of questions are based only on figures.

EXAMPLE 1 Which is the correct water image from the given four images?

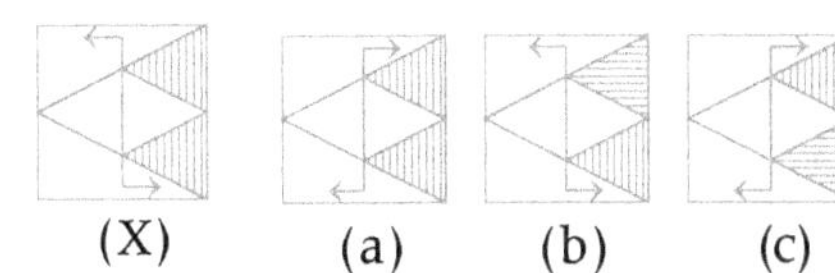

(X) (a) (b) (c) (d)

Sol. (a)

Hence, option (a) is correct.

Alphabet Based

In this type of questions are based only on Alphabets.

EXAMPLE 2 Select the correct water image of given word.

N A T I O N

(a) N A ⊥ I O И (b) И A T I O И
(c) И ∀ ⊥ I O И (d) И ∀ ⊥ I O N

Sol. (c) Correct water image is shown below as

N A T I O N
Water
И ∀ ⊥ I O И

Hence, option (c) is correct.

Number Based

In this type of questions are based only on numbers.

Example 3 Choose the correct water image of the given number.

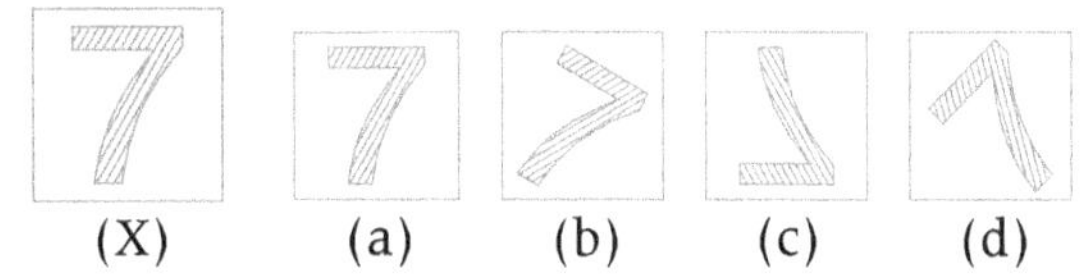

(X) (a) (b) (c) (d)

Sol. (c) The correct water image is as shown below:

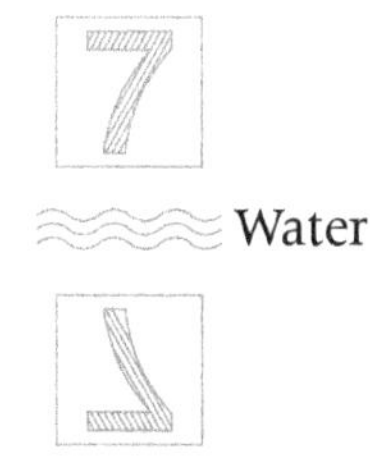

Hence, option (c) is correct.

Let's Practice

1 Mark Questions

Directions (Q. Nos. 1-13) In each of the following questions, find out the correct water image of the given object (X).

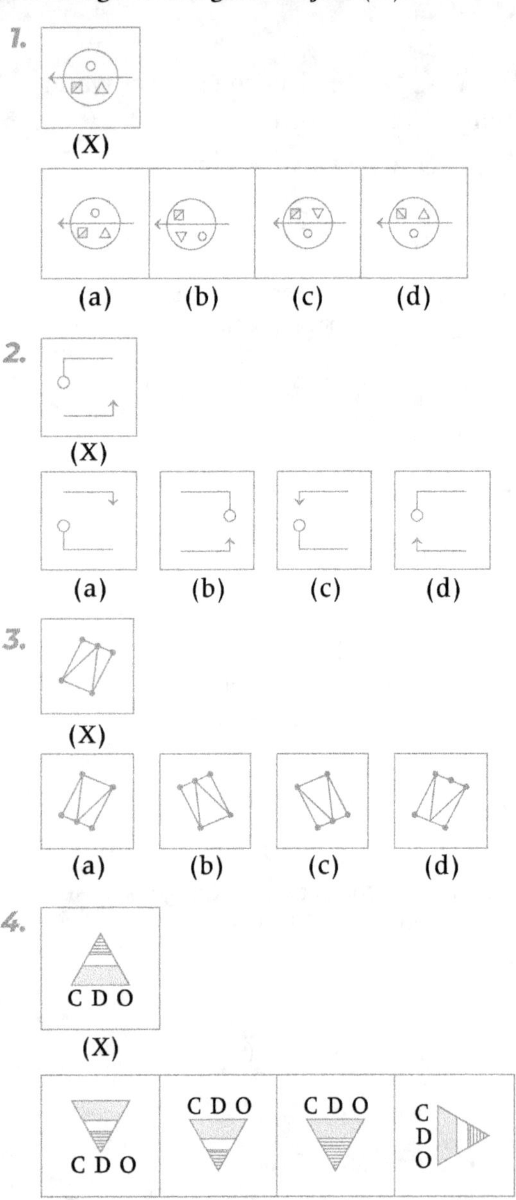

5.

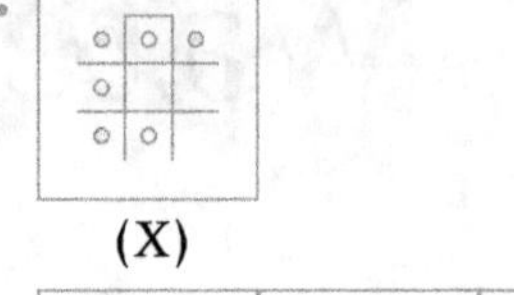

(X)

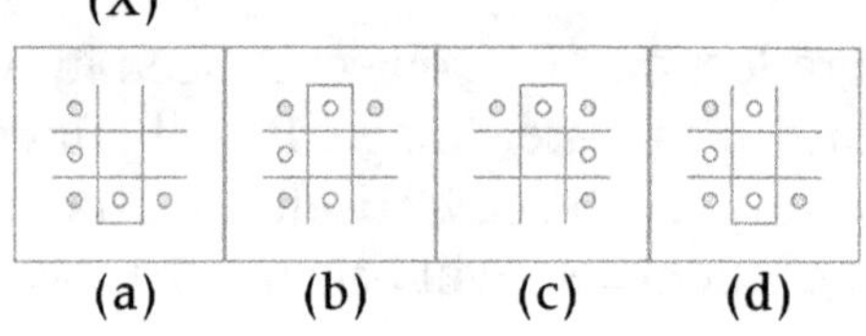

(a) (b) (c) (d)

6.

(X)

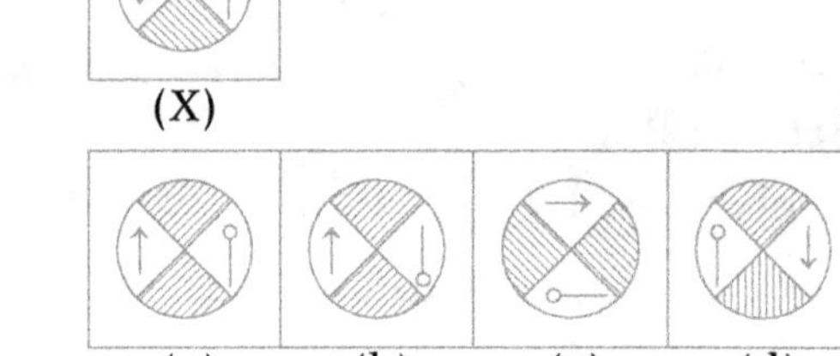

(a) (b) (c) (d)

7.

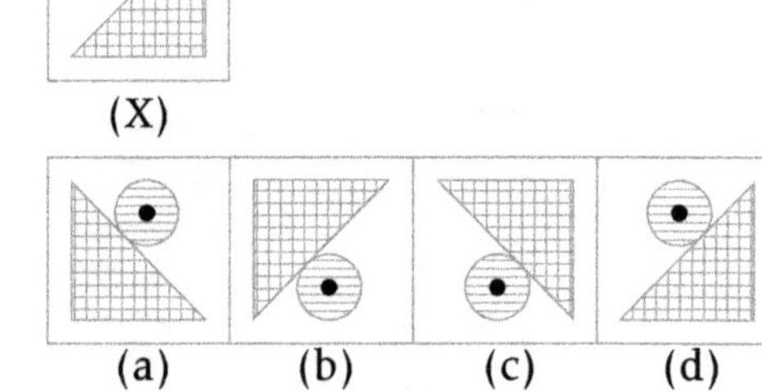

(X)

(a) (b) (c) (d)

8.

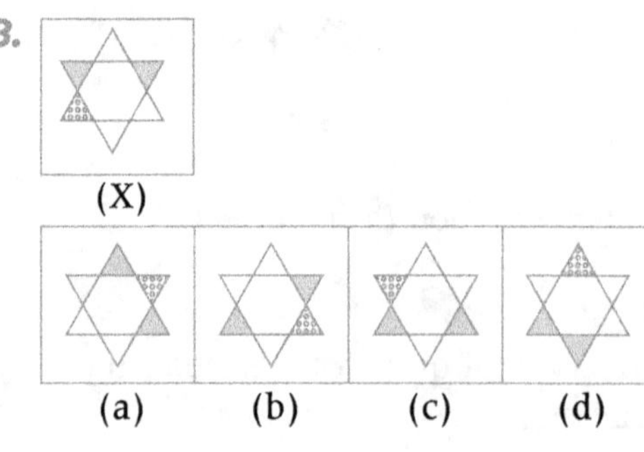

(X)

(a) (b) (c) (d)

9\.

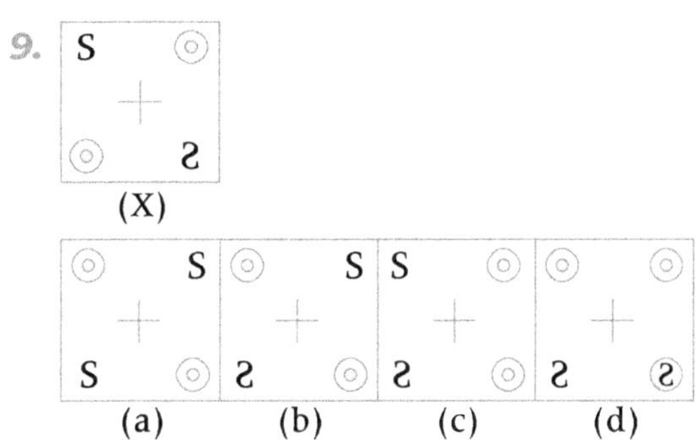

(X)

(a) (b) (c) (d)

Directions (Q. Nos. 10 and 11) In each of the following questions, choose the correct water image of the given letters.

10\. TAMNCZ

(a) ⊥ꓯWNƆZ (b) TVMИCZ

(c) ⊥VWИCZ (d) TAWNCZ

11\. monday

(a) yadnom (b) yɒbnom

(c) ʎɐqnoɯ (d) ɯouqɐʎ

Directions (Q. Nos. 12 and 13) In each of the following questions, choose the correct water image of the given number.

12\. 43867

(a) ⱶ38ə7 (b) 4386⅃

(c) ⱶƐ8ə7 (d) ꟻ38୧⅃

13\. 859431

(a) 82əꟻ3I

(b) 85əꟻ31

(c) 829ꟻ31

(d) 859ꟻ3I

2 Marks Questions

Directions (Q. Nos. 14-16) Choose the correct water image of the given figure.

14\.

(X)

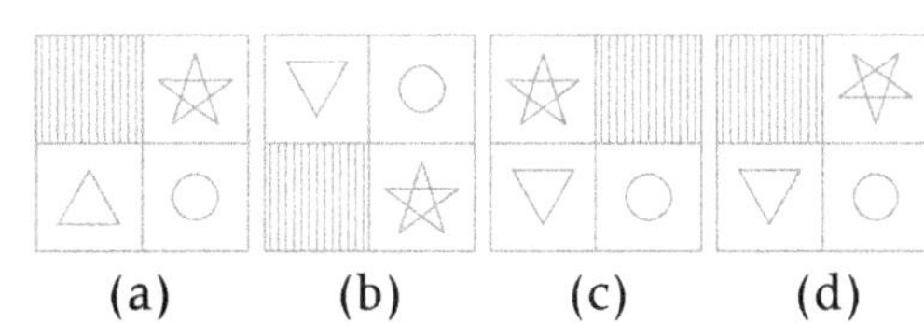

(a) (b) (c) (d)

15\.

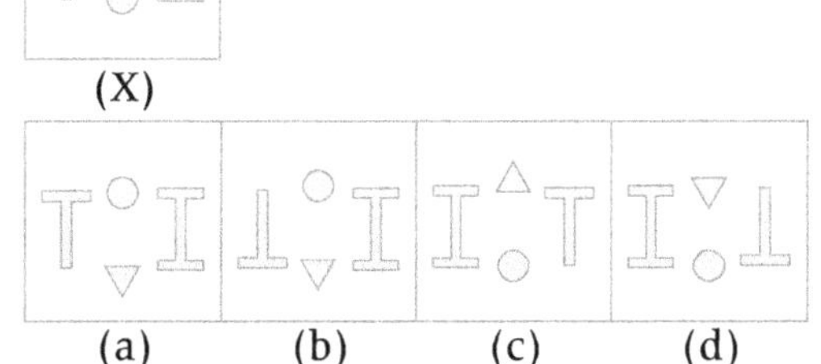

(X)

(a) (b) (c) (d)

16\.

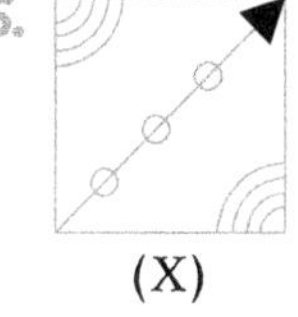

(X)

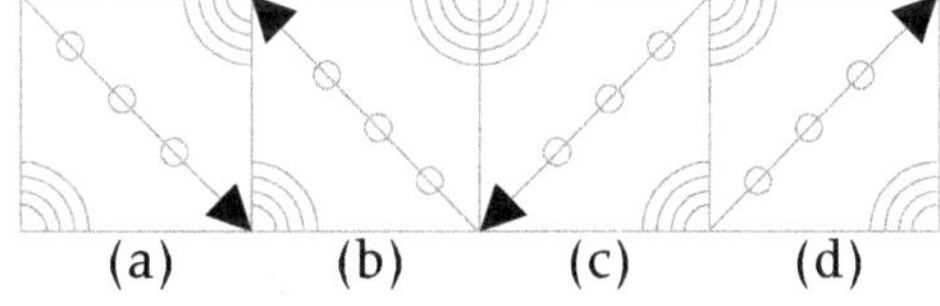

(a) (b) (c) (d)

17\. Select the correct water image of the given word.

BEHAVE

(a) ꓭEHAVE (b) ꓭƎHAVE

(c) ꓭEHVVE (d) BEHVΛE

18\. Find the correct water image of the given number.

S987356S

(a) Sə873262 (b) 298⅃32୧2

(c) S98⅃3562 (d) 2ə8⅃32୧2

Chapter 14

Paper Folding and Paper Cutting

'Paper Folding and Paper Cutting' problems are based on a sheet of paper which is folded along a dotted line or cut (punched) in a particular manner.

Paper Folding

Paper folding involves selection of a figure which would most closely resemble the pattern that would be formed when a transparent sheet carrying certain designs on either sides of a dotted line, is folded along the line.

EXAMPLE 1 In the following question, a transparent sheet having certain design on either sides of dotted line is given. The figure is followed by four answer figures and one out of these is obtained by folding the transparent sheet along the dotted line. Choose the correct option.

Transparent Sheet

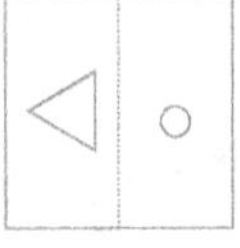

Answer Sheets

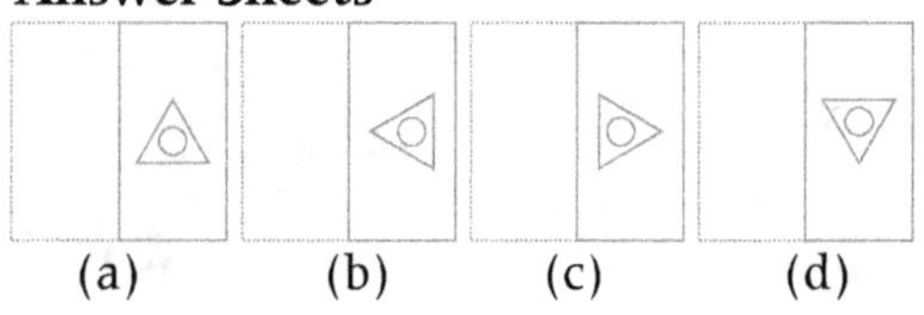

(a) (b) (c) (d)

Sol. (c) The folded transparent sheet will appear as adjacent figure.

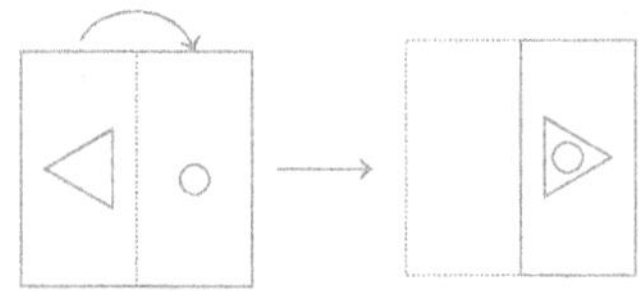

Hence, option (c) is correct.

Paper Cutting

In paper cutting a piece of paper is folded twice or thrice in certain directions indicated by the arrows and then cuts are made into it. Students are required to determine the pattern which will be formed when the sheet is unfolded.

EXAMPLE 2 In the following question, a set of three figures showing a sequence in which a paper is folded and cut in a particular manner. You have to select the answer figure. Showing the design which the paper actually acquires when it is unfolded.

Transparent Sheets

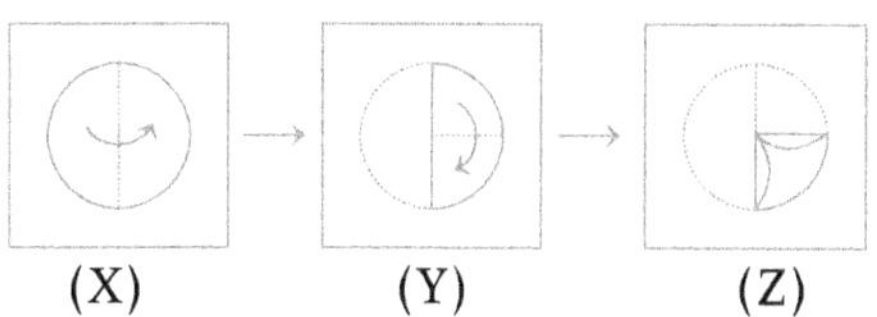

(X) (Y) (Z)

Answer Figures

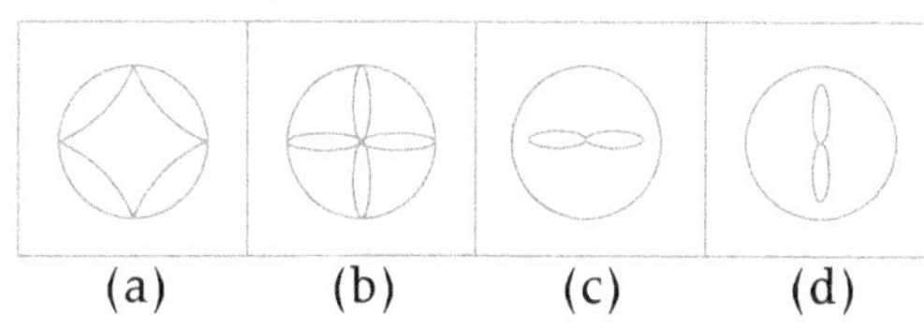

(a) (b) (c) (d)

Sol. (b)When the first fold is opened the paper will look like as

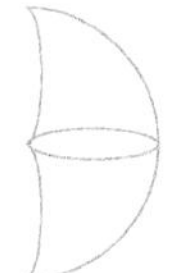

Now, when the paper is unfolded completely it will look like as

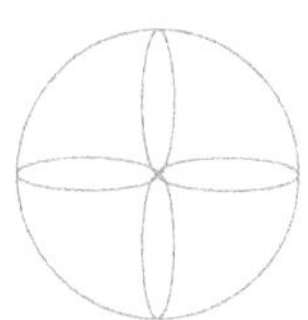

Hence, option (b) is correct.

Let's Practice

1 Mark Questions

Directions (Q. Nos. 1-5) In each of the following questions, a transparent sheet having certain design on either sides of dotted line is given. One out of these four alternatives is obtained by folding the transparent sheet along the dotted line. Choose the correct option.

1. **Transparent Sheet**

Answer Sheets

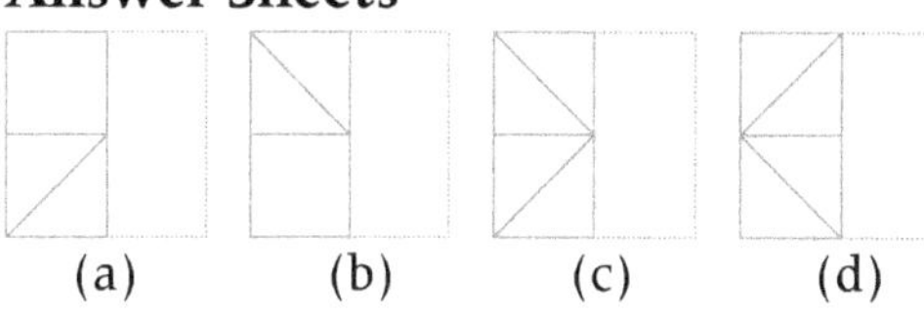

(a) (b) (c) (d)

2. **Transparent Sheet**

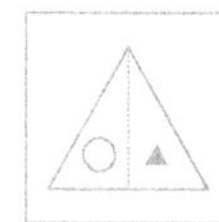

Answer Sheets

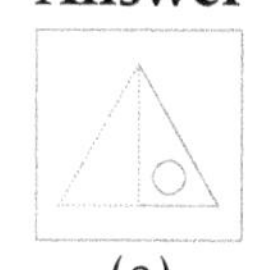

(a) (b) (c) (d)

3. **Transparent Sheet**

Answer Sheets

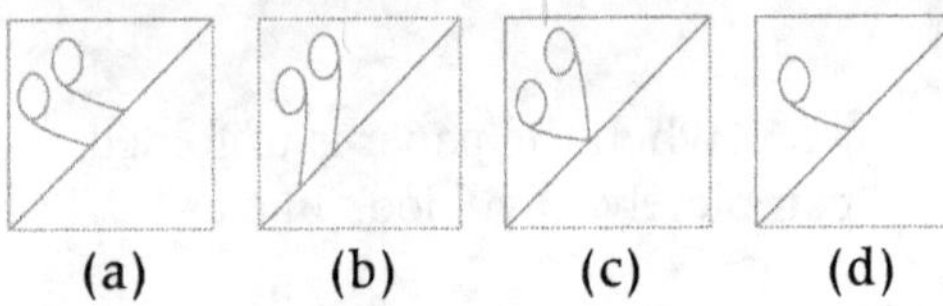

(a) (b) (c) (d)

4. **Transparent Sheet**

Answer Sheets

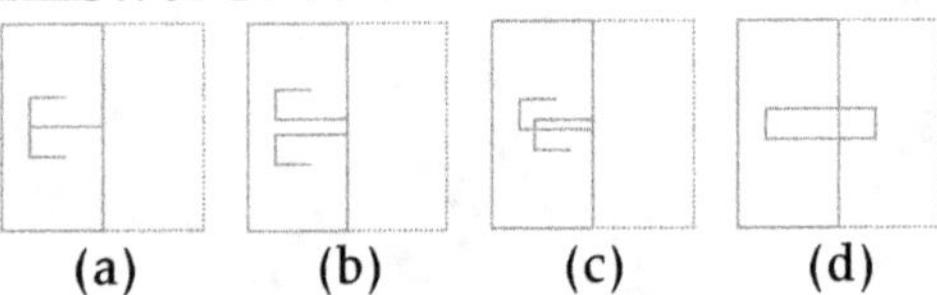

(a) (b) (c) (d)

5. **Transparent Sheet**

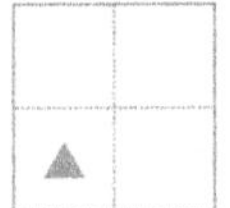

Answer Sheets

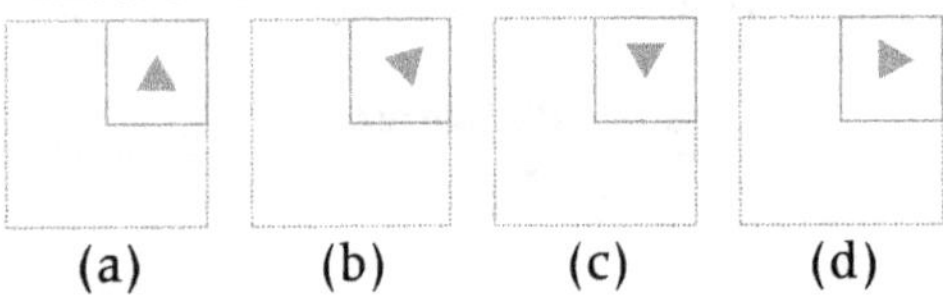

(a) (b) (c) (d)

Directions (Q. Nos. 6-8) In each of the following questions, a set of three figures is given, showing a sequence in which a paper is folded and finally cut in a particular manner. Now, you have to select the answer figure, showing the design which the paper actually acquires when it is unfolded.

6. **Transparent Sheets**

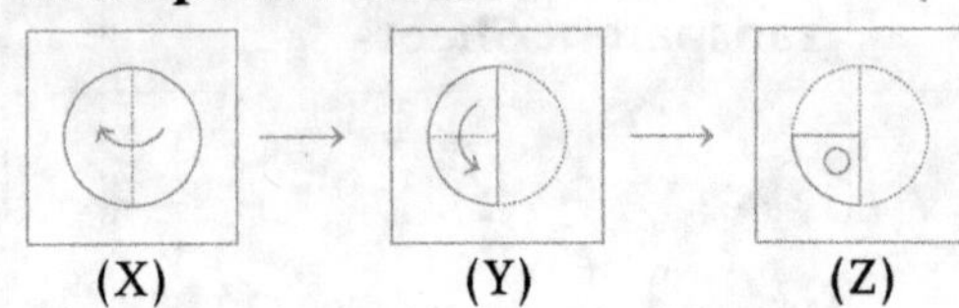

(X) (Y) (Z)

Answer Sheets

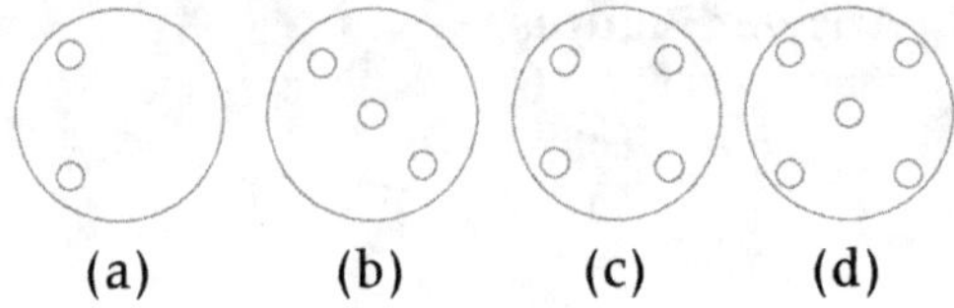

(a) (b) (c) (d)

7. **Transparent Sheets**

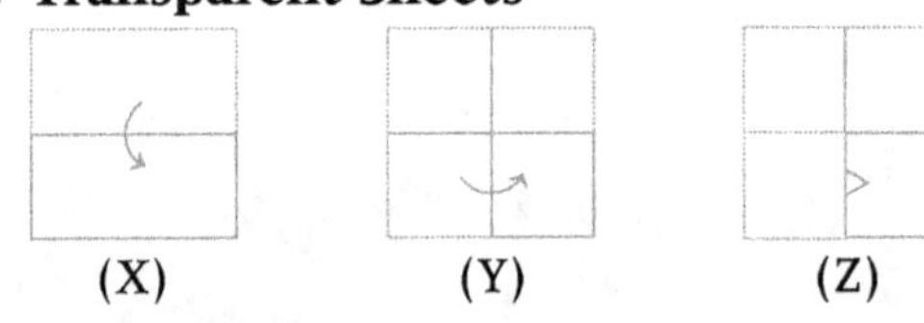

(X) (Y) (Z)

Answer Sheets

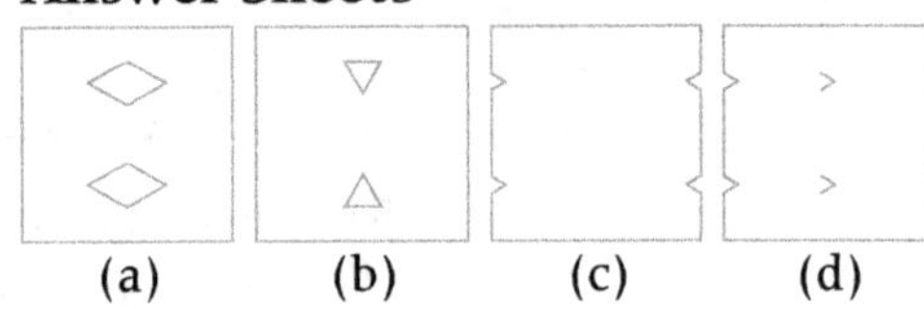

(a) (b) (c) (d)

8. **Transparent Sheets**

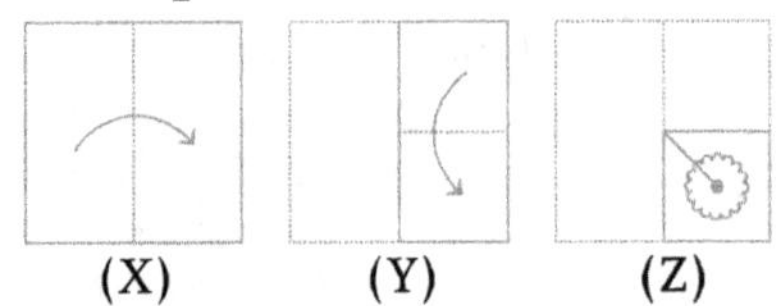

(X) (Y) (Z)

Answer Sheets

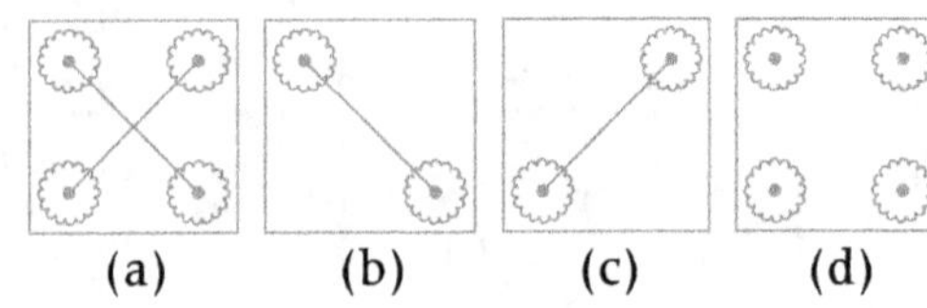

(a) (b) (c) (d)

2 Marks Questions

Directions (Q. Nos. 9 and 10) In each of the following questions, a transparent sheet having certain design on either sides of dotted line is given. One out of these four alternatives is obtained by folding the transparent sheet along the dotted line. Choose the correct option.

9. **Transparent Sheet**

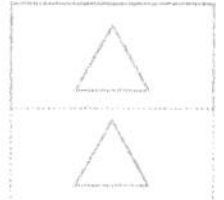

Answer Sheets

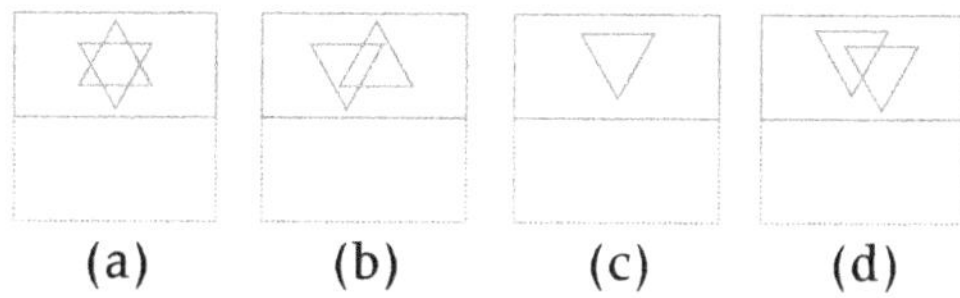

(a) (b) (c) (d)

10. **Transparent Sheet**

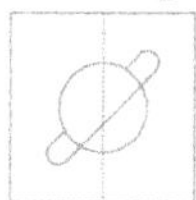

Answer Sheets

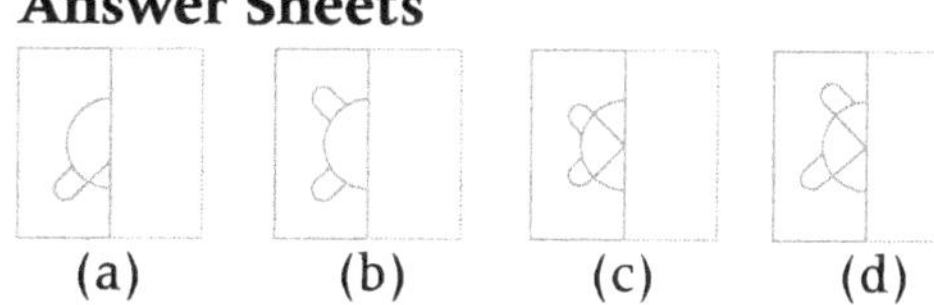

(a) (b) (c) (d)

Directions (Q. Nos. 11-12) In each of the following questions, a set of three figures is given, showing a sequence in which a paper is folded and finally cut in a particular manner.

Now, you have to select the answer figure, showing the design which the paper actually acquires when it is unfolded.

11. **Transparent Sheets**

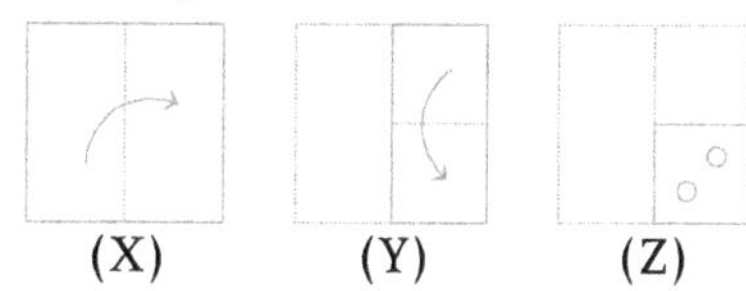

(X) (Y) (Z)

Answer Sheets

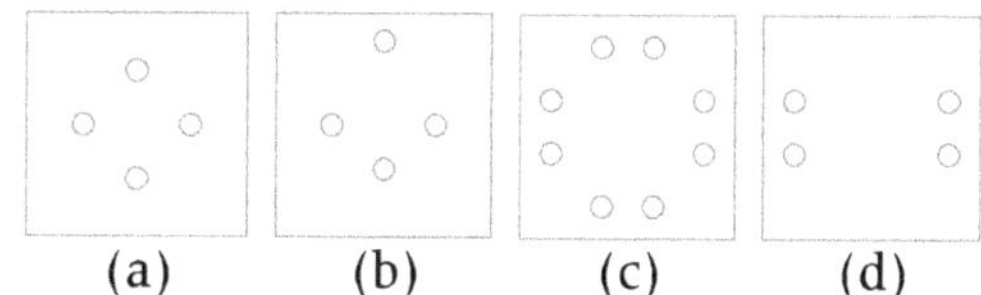

(a) (b) (c) (d)

12. **Transparent Sheets**

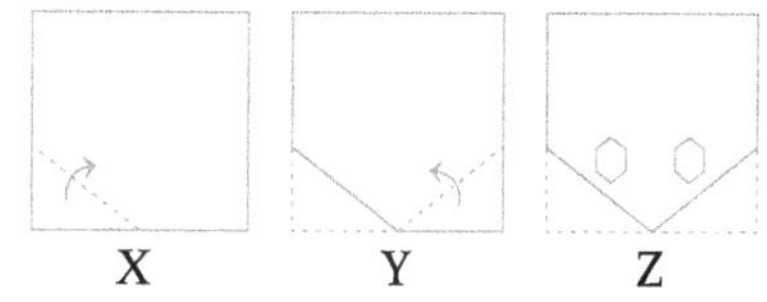

X Y Z

Answer Sheets

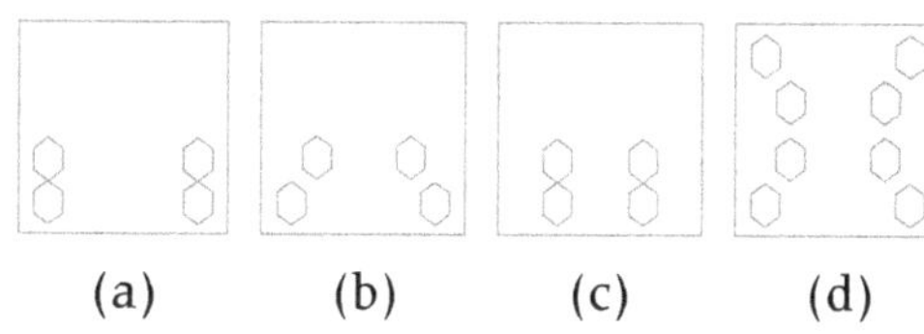

(a) (b) (c) (d)

Embedded Figures and Figure Formation

Embedded figure refers to a simple geometrical figure which is present or hidden in other large or complex figure.

Here, a figure is said to be embedded in another figure when the second figure completely contains the first figure.

In embedded figures, following types of questions are generally asked.

EXAMPLE 1 Find out the alternative figure which contains figure (X) as its part.

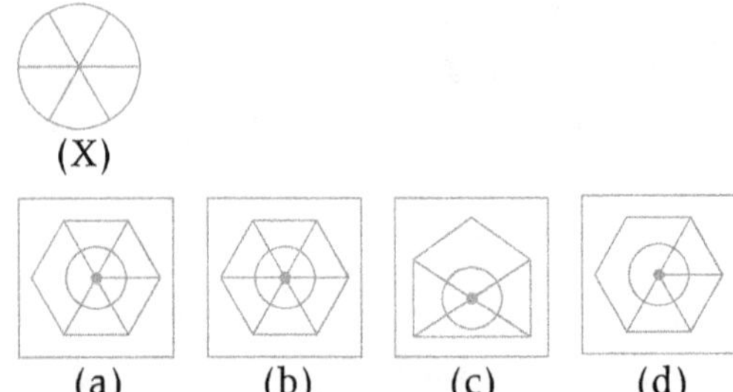

Sol. (b) After close observation, we find that figure (X) is exactly embedded in figure (b) as shown below:

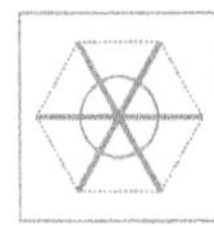

Hence, option (b) is correct.

Figure Formation and Analysis

In figure formation, geometrical figures such as triangle, squares and rectangles etc. are formed by joining two or more than two components and we also identify identical figures or components of the given figure from a given set of figures.

EXAMPLE 2 Which of the following shapes, when fitted to the piece in figure. (X) will form a perfect square?

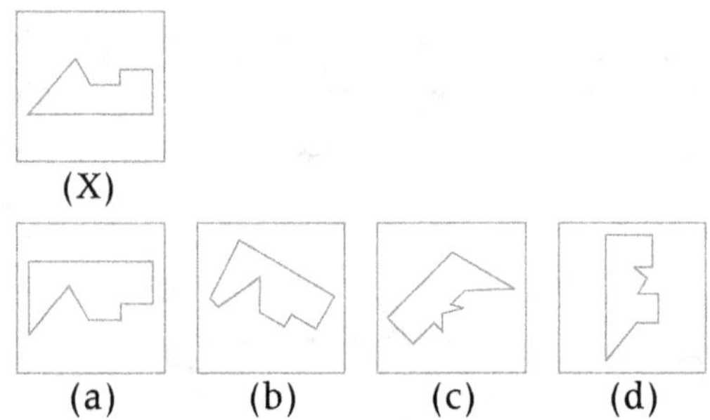

Sol. (a) It is clear from the given options that figure (a) will form the square when join with figure (X) as shown below:

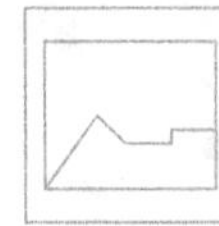

Hence, option (a) is correct.

In grouping of identical figures such type of problems question based on a set of some figures.

EXAMPLE 3 Group the following figures into three classes on the basis of identical properties.

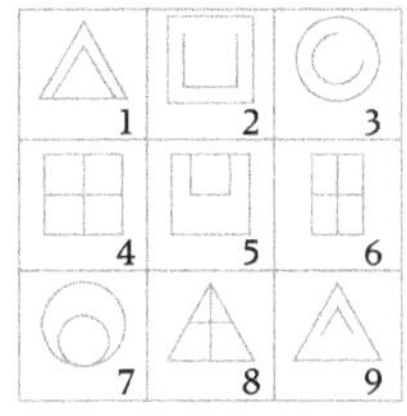

(a) 1, 5, 7; 2, 3, 9; 4, 6, 8
(b) 1, 3, 9; 2, 4, 6; 5, 7, 8
(c) 2, 4, 5; 9, 1, 3; 7, 8, 6
(d) 3, 2, 1; 4, 6, 5; 9, 7, 8

Sol. (a) From the above figures, it is clear that figures (1), (5) and (7) follow same property with two similar shapes. In figures (2), (3) and (9), the object has incomplete figure inside it and in figures (4), (6) and (8) each figure is divided into four parts.

Thus, the given nine figures may be divided into three groups as (1, 5, 7); (2, 3, 9); (4, 6, 8).

Hence, option (a) is correct.

Let's Practice

1 Mark Questions

Directions (Q. Nos. 1-4) In the following questions, a question figure (X) and a set of four answer figures (a), (b), (c) and (d) are given. Find out answer figure in which the question figure (X) is embedded.

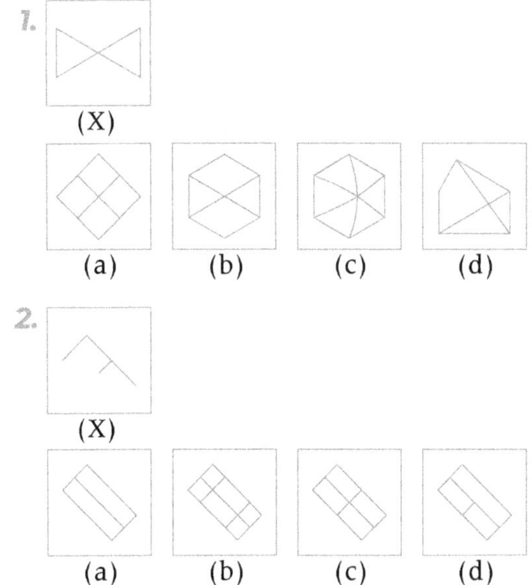

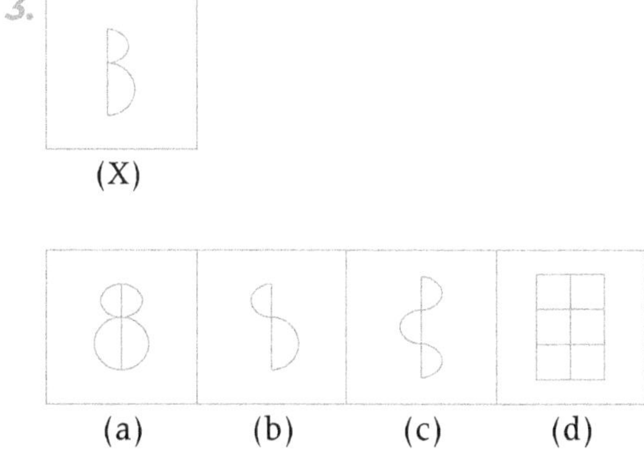

Directions (Q. Nos. 4 and 5) In each of the following questions find out the figure from the answer figures, that can be formed by joining the pieces given in the question figure.

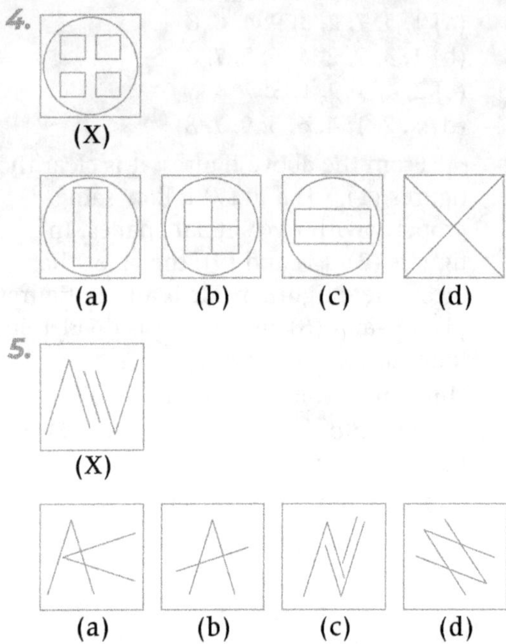

Directions (Q. Nos. 6 and 7) In each of the following questions, select the option in which all the components of the question figure (X) are available.

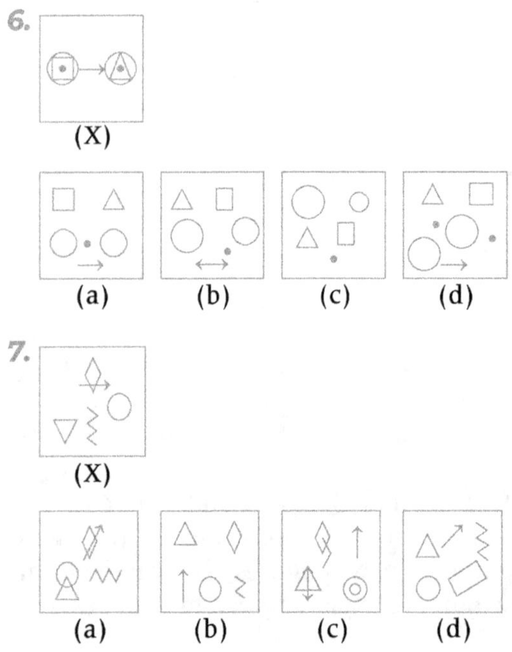

Directions (Q. Nos. 8-10) In each of the following questions, question figure (X) is given followed by other four alternative figures. It is required to select one figure from the alternatives, which exactly fits into figure (X), to form a perfect square.

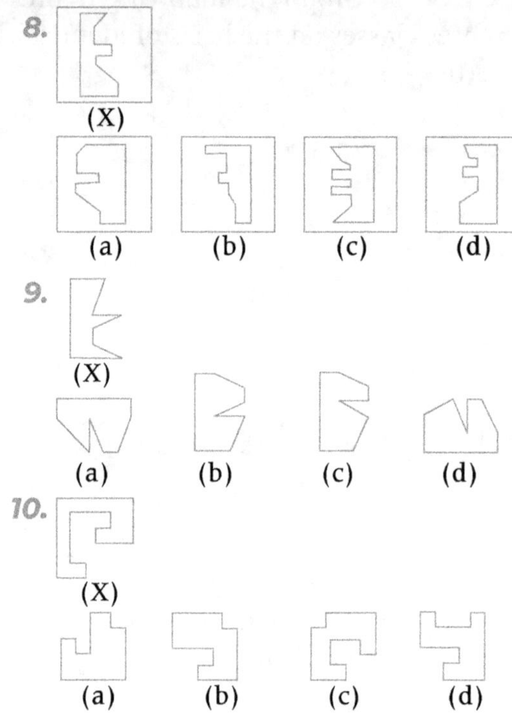

Directions (Q. Nos. 11-13) In each of the following questions, group the given figures into three classes using each figure only once.

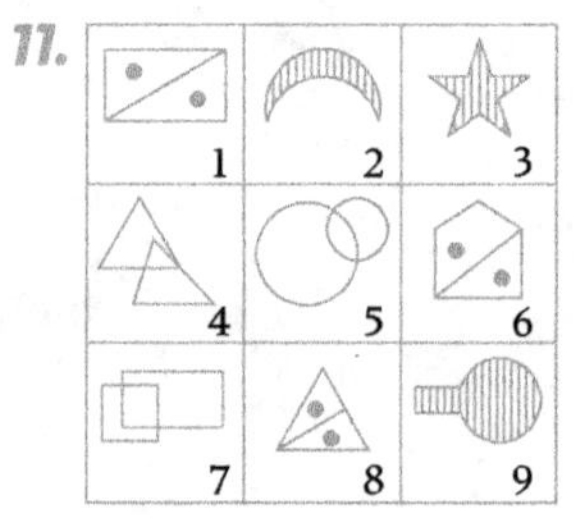

(a) 1, 2, 3; 5, 8, 9; 4, 6, 7
(b) 1, 6, 8; 2, 3, 9; 4, 5, 7
(c) 1, 5, 9; 2, 6, 7; 3, 8, 4
(d) 1, 5, 7; 4, 3, 8; 2, 6, 9

12. 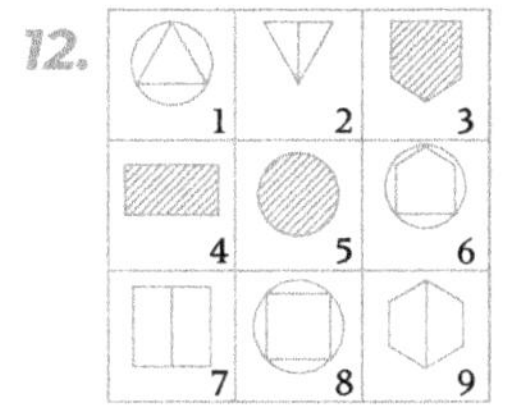

(a) 9, 4, 8; 3, 6, 7; 1, 2, 5
(b) 1, 2, 4; 7, 9, 5; 8, 6, 3
(c) 1, 8, 6; 2, 7, 9; 3, 5, 4
(d) 5, 3, 2; 4, 6, 9; 1, 7, 8

13. 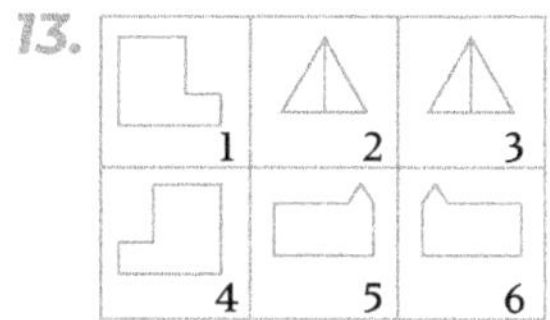

(a) 1,4 ; 2,3 ; 5,6
(b) 1,5 ; 2,6 ; 4,3
(c) 1,6 ; 2,3 ; 4,5
(d) 1,2 ; 3,6 ; 4,5

2 Marks Questions

Directions (Q. Nos. 14 and 15) In the following questions, a question figure (X) and a set of four answer figures (a), (b), (c) and (d) are given. Find out answer figure in which the question figure (X) is embedded.

14. 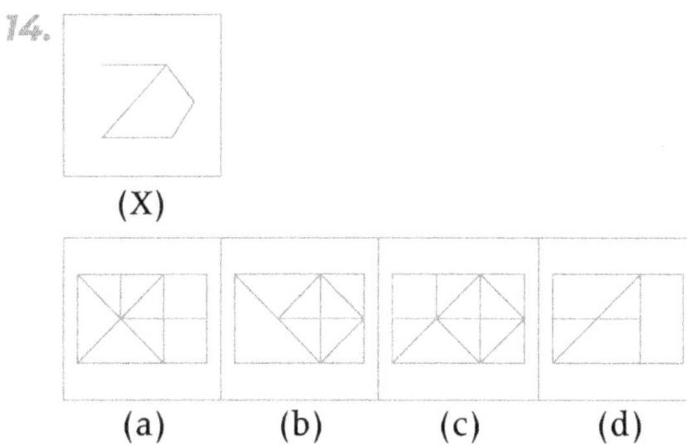

15. 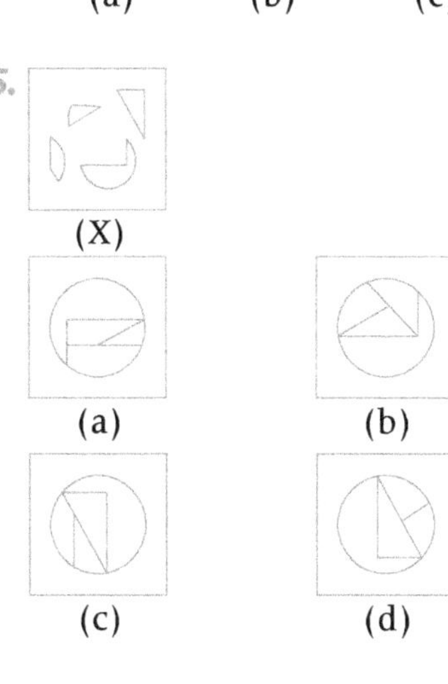

Direction (Q. No. 16) In each of the following questions, select the option in which all the components of the question figure (X) are available.

16. 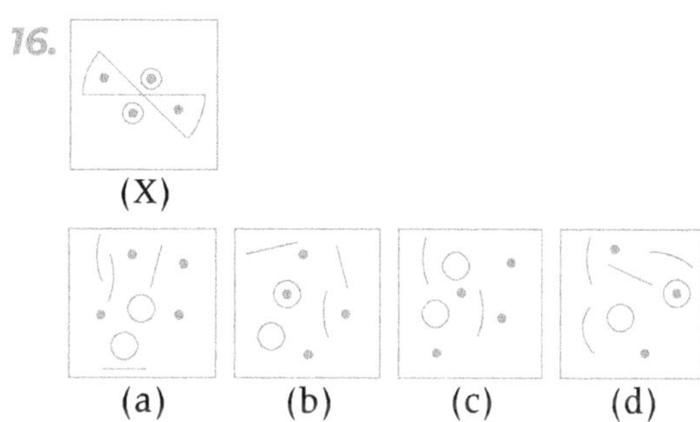

Directions (Q. Nos. 17 and 18) In each of the following questions, question figure (X) is given followed by other four alternative figures. It is required to select one figure from the alternatives, which exactly fits into figure (X), to form a perfect square.

17. 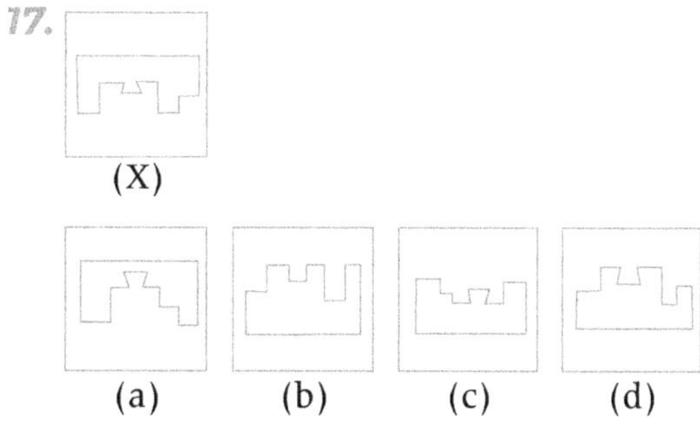

18.

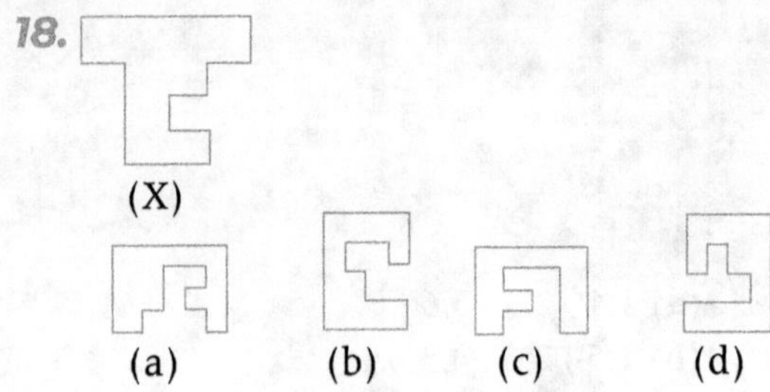

Direction (Q. No. 19) In each of the following question, group the given figures into three classes using each figure only once.

19.

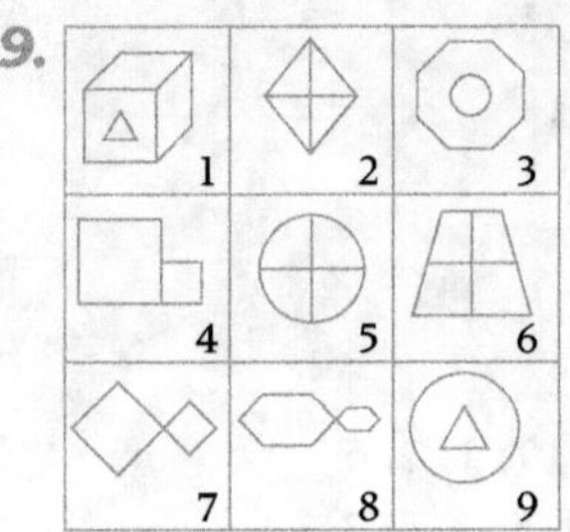

(a) 1,3,9 ; 2,5,6 ; 4,7,8
(b) 1,3,9 ; 2,7,8 ; 4,5,6
(c) 1,2,4 ; 3,5,7 ; 6,8,9
(d) 1,3,6 ; 2,4,8 ; 5,7,9

PRACTICE SET 

1 Mark Questions

1. Find the next term in the series.
   7 11 17 25 35 ?
   (a) 45 b 47 (c) 49 d 51

2. HJL is related to JMP, in the same way as OQS is related to
   (a) PSV (b) MHJ (c) QTW (d) RUX

3. Which number will replace the question mark?
   8 — 3 — 4 , 10 — 5 — 10 , 15 — ? — 9
   (a) 6 (b) 4 (c) 8 (d) 42

4. Select the correct mirror image of the following.
   NAME25
   (a) ИAMƎƧƧ (b) ƧƧƎMAИ (c) ƧƧƎWAИ (d) ƧƧMƎИA

5. If '×' means '÷', '+' means '×', '–' means '+' and '÷' means '×', then
   $125 \times 25 + 20 - 80 = ?$
   (a) 180 (b) 90 (c) 200 (d) 20

6. If 'X' is the wife of 'Y', 'Y' is the brother of 'Z' and 'P' is the father of 'Z', then how is 'P' related to 'X'?
   (a) Aunt (b) Brother
   (c) Father-in-law (d) Sister

7. Which figure completes the second pair in the same way as first pair?
   : :: : ?
   (a) (b) (c) (d)

8. Choose the figure which is different from others.
   (a) 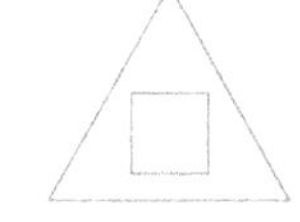
   (b) 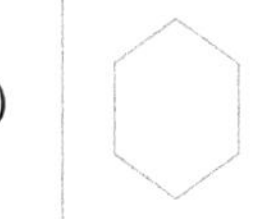
   (c) 
   (d)

9. Five children are sitting on a bench. P is to the left of Q and to the right of R. S is to the right of Q. T is between Q and S. Then, whose position is fourth from the right?
   (a) R (b) Q
   (c) S (d) P

10. Find the one which does not belong to the group.
    (a) Tail (b) Hale
    (c) Nail (d) Sail

11. If the following transparent sheet with a certain design is folded along the dotted line, then how will it appear

(X)

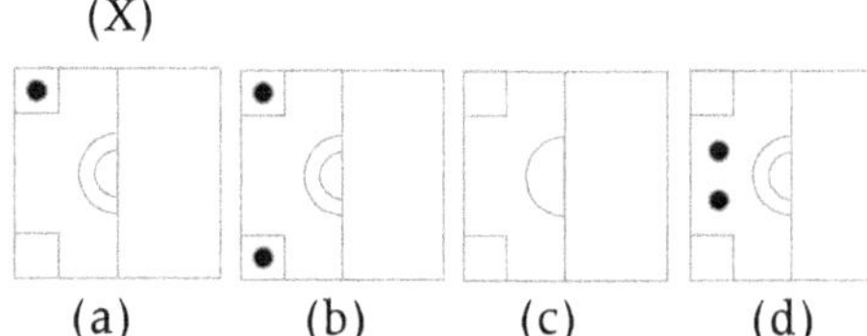

(a) (b) (c) (d)

12. In which of the following options, Figure (X) is embedded as its part?

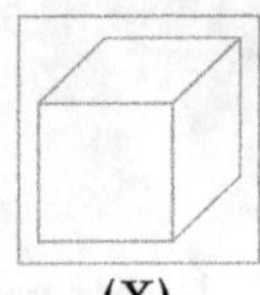

(X)

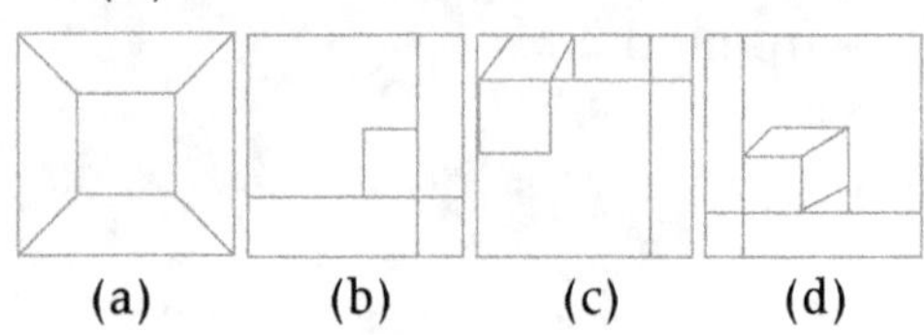

(a) (b) (c) (d)

13. Ram is facing East. He turn 135° in clockwise direction and then 180° in anti-clockwise direction. Which direction he is facing now?

(a) East (b) North
(c) North-East (d) South-West

14. If in a certain code, HAPPY is coded as YPPAH, how is TEACH coded in that code?

(a) HCAET (b) AETHC
(c) EACTH (d) HCEAT

15. 'Chapter' is related to 'Book', in the same way as Brick is related to

(a) Clay (b) Mud
(c) Building (d) Mason

16. Find the odd one out.

(a) 

(b) G K I

(c) 

(d) H L J

17. What comes next in the series given below?

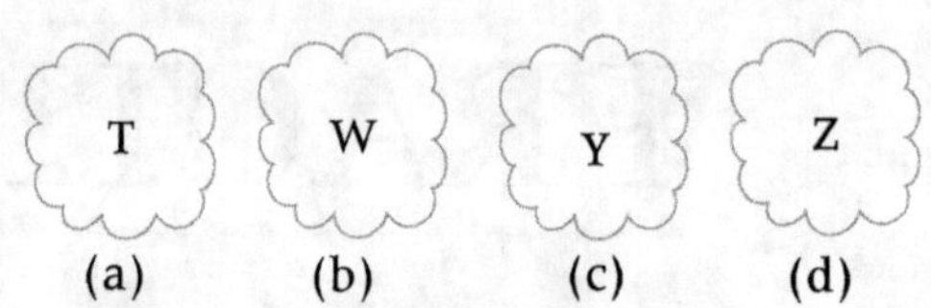

(a) (b) (c) (d)

18. If SLOW is coded as 1598 and TAKE is coded as 2437, then LATE is coded as

9247	5427	5834	7594
(a)	(b)	(c)	(d)

19. Find the missing number in the following figure.

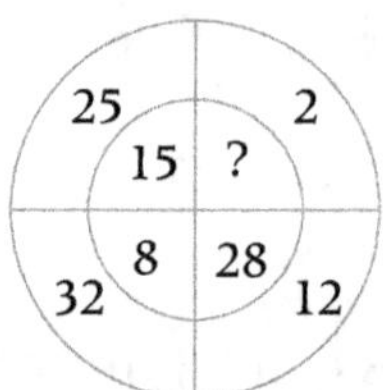

(a) 38 (b) 14
(c) 28 (d) 30

20. The letters of the words given in each of the four options have been jumbled up. Identify the word in the options for the clue given below.

Synonym of 'Heal'.

(a) CUQIK (b) AEBRK
(c) GMDAAE (d) UCER

21. If 7 * 8 = 56, 6 * 9 = 54 and 4 * 6 = 24, then find the value of 11 * 5.

(a) 55 (b) 40
(c) 50 (d) 44

22. Akanksha moves 8 km towards West, then 2 km towards South and then 6 km towards East. Find the total distance covered by Akanksha.

(a) 18 km (b) 16 km
(c) 4 km (d) 6 km

23. Ashwini said pointing towards Sachin, "He is my sister's only brother's Son". How is Sachin related to Ashwini?

(a) Father (b) Brother
(c) Son (d) Uncle

24. Arrange the following words according to English dictionary.

1. Hepatitis 2. Cholera
3. Peptidoglycan 4. Chitin

(a) 2, 3, 1, 4 (b) 4, 2, 1, 3
(c) 4, 1, 3, 2 (d) 3, 1, 4, 2

25. Find the next figure in the series given below.

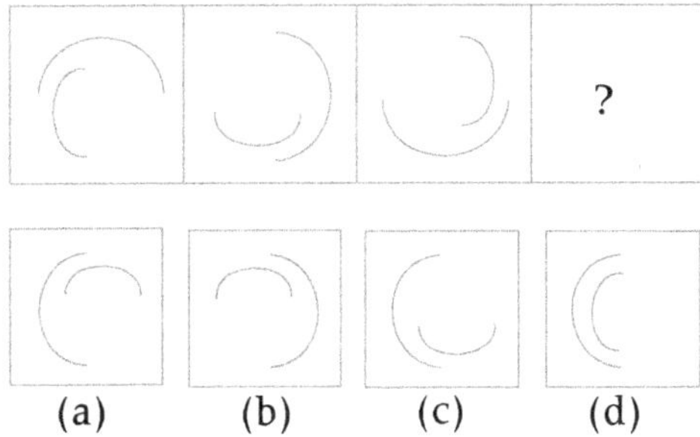

(a) (b) (c) (d)

26. Complete the second pair in the same way as first pair.

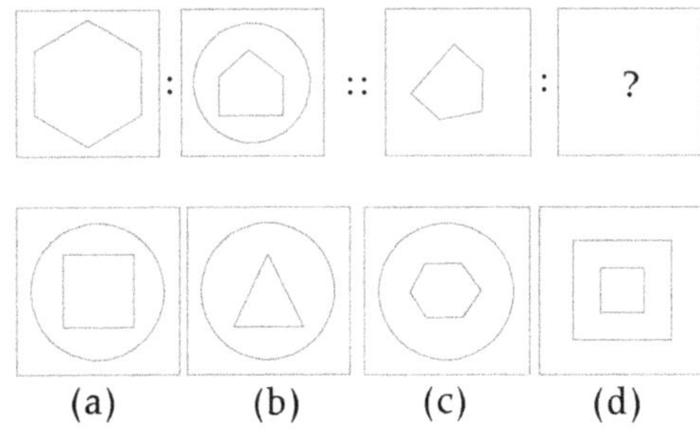

(a) (b) (c) (d)

27. In the following question, a problem figure is given followed by four answer figures. You have to choose that answer figure which on joining will make a complete square with the problem figurc.

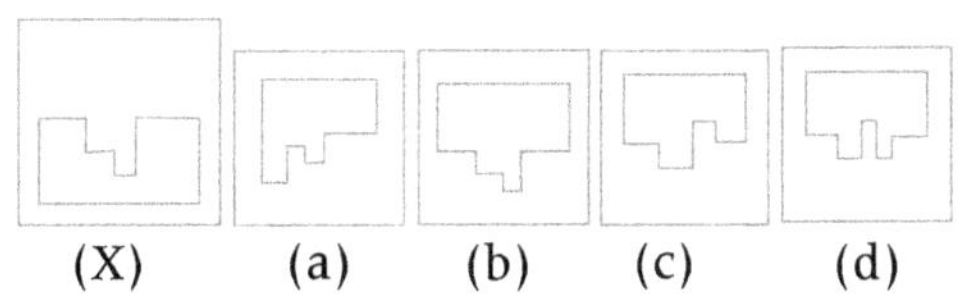

(X) (a) (b) (c) (d)

28. Find the pattern which will appear on the transparent sheet after it is folded along the dotted line.

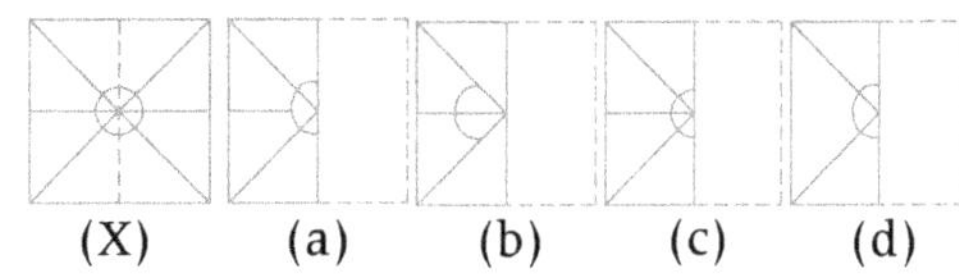

(X) (a) (b) (c) (d)

29. Select the correct mirror image of the figure given below.

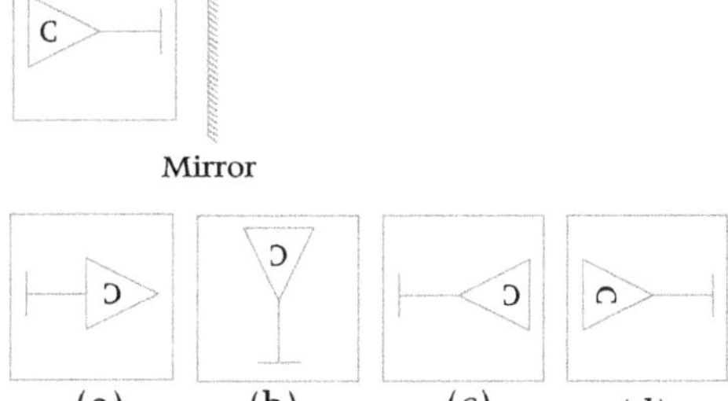

(a) (b) (c) (d)

30. If P = 14, Q = 4, R = 8 and S = 2, then $Q + R + S = ?$

(a) Q (b) R (c) P (d) S

31. Choose the odd one out.

(a) BC (b) KM (c) GH (d) WX

32. (A) (B) (D) (G) (K) (?)

(a) P (b) Q (c) R (d) L

33. 28 is related to 10, in the same way 63 is related to

(a) 6 (b) 7 (c) 8 (d) 9

34. Vamika walks 40 m towards North. Then she turns left and walks 60 m. She again turns and walks 40 m. Further, she moves 40 m after turning to the right. How far is she from her original position?

(a) 40 m (b) 50 m (c) 70 m (d) 100 m

35. If RESANO is coded as S1T203, then MORALE is coded as
(a) 3N2S1M (b) NSM123
(c) 123NSM (d) N3S2MI

36. How many three letter meaningful words can be formed from the word 'TEAR' beginning with 'A' and without repeating any letter within that word?
(a) One (b) Two (c) Three (d) Four

37. Find out the correct water image of the figure (X).

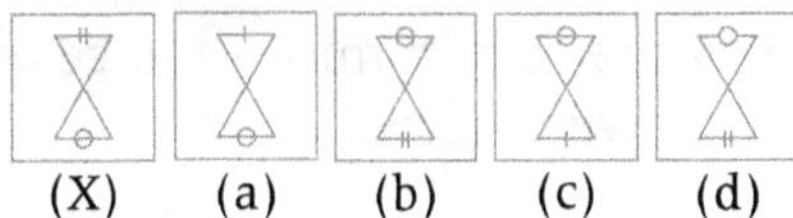

(X) (a) (b) (c) (d)

38. Nitin ranks eighteenth in a class of 49 students. What is his rank from the last?
(a) 18 (b) 19 (c) 31 (d) 32

39. Find the missing number.

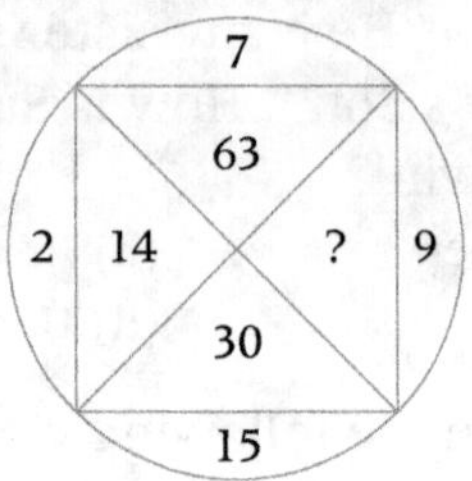

(a) 18 (b) 33
(c) 135 (d) 145

40. Find the mirror image of the given word.

FIXING

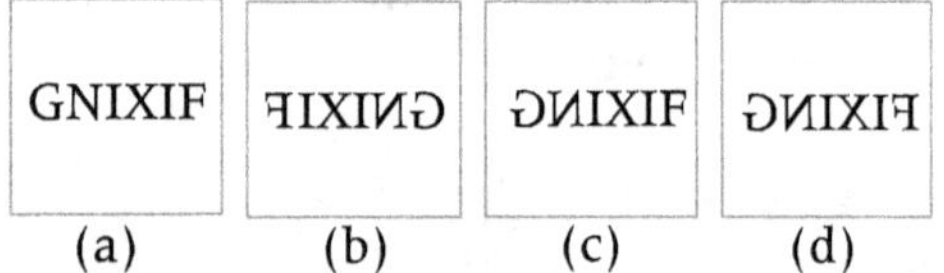

(a) (b) (c) (d)

2 Mark Questions

41. The letter of the words given in each of the four options have been jumbled up. Identify the word in the option for the clue given below.

'A day of a week'

(a) ACMRH (b) AOTDY
(c) OMDANY (d) LOHIYAD

42. Find the next figure in the series given below.

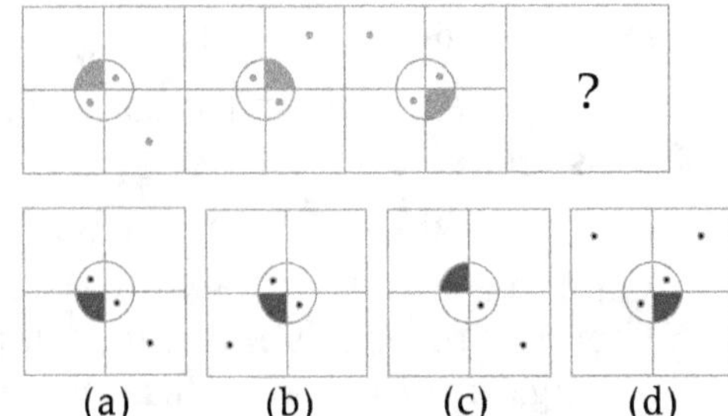

(a) (b) (c) (d)

43. Consider the figures (X) and (Y) showing a sheet of paper folded and punched in Figure (Z). Select the figure, which will most closely resemble the unfolded form of figure?

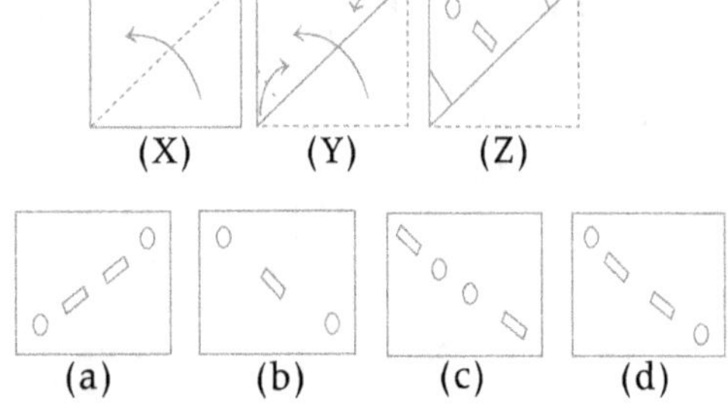

(X) (Y) (Z)

(a) (b) (c) (d)

44. Read the following information carefully and answer the question given below.
Raghu and Gyan are good players in cricket and hockey. Sohan and Gyan are good players in hockey and chess. Raghu and Govind are good players in swimming and cricket.
Who is good in cricket, hockey and chess?
(a) Raghu (b) Gyan (c) Sohan (d) Govind

45. Choose the Figure which is different from others.

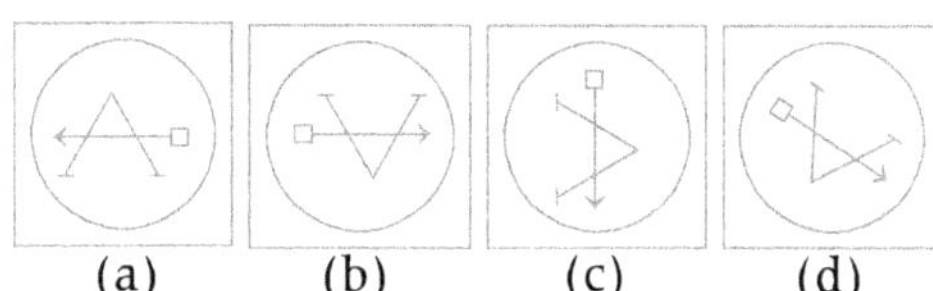

(a) (b) (c) (d)

46. In a joint family, there are father, mother, 3 married sons and one unmarried daughter. Of the sons, two have 2 daughters each, and one has a son. How many female members are there in the family?

(a) 2 (b) 3
(c) 6 (d) 9

47. Rahul is facing towards East and turns through 45° clockwise and then turns through 90° anti-clockwise. In which direction is he facing now?

(a) North-West (b) North-East
(c) East (d) South-East

48. Find the next Figure in the series given below.

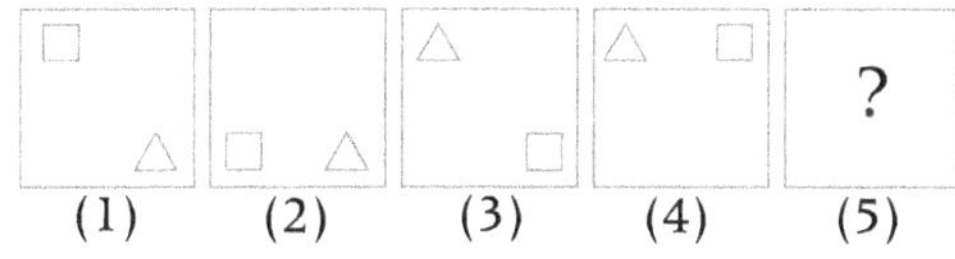

(1) (2) (3) (4) (5)

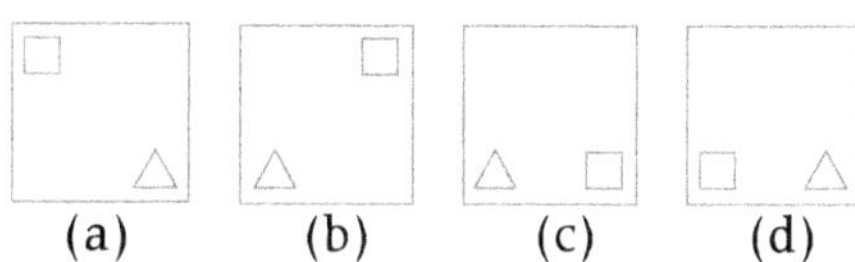

(a) (b) (c) (d)

49. If the given interchanges are made in signs and numbers, which one of the four equations would be correct?

Given interchanges : Signs '+' and '−'
Given interchanges : 12 and 24

(a) $12 \div 24 - 36 = 48$ (b) $12 - 24 + 36 = 0$
(c) $24 \div 12 - 36 = 72$ (d) $24 - 12 \div 36 = 24$

50. In the given figure matrix which option figure will replace the question mark (?)?

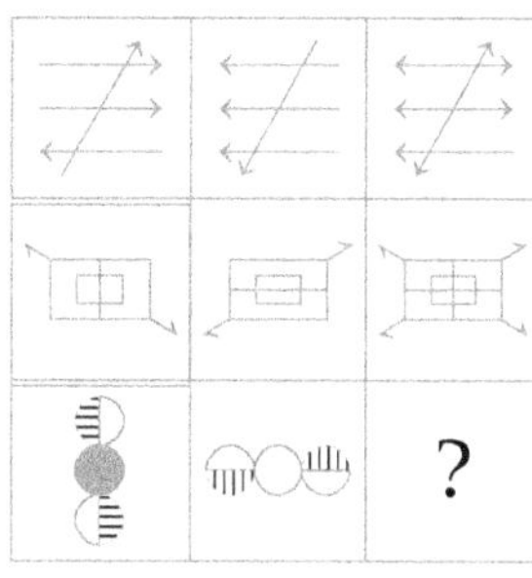

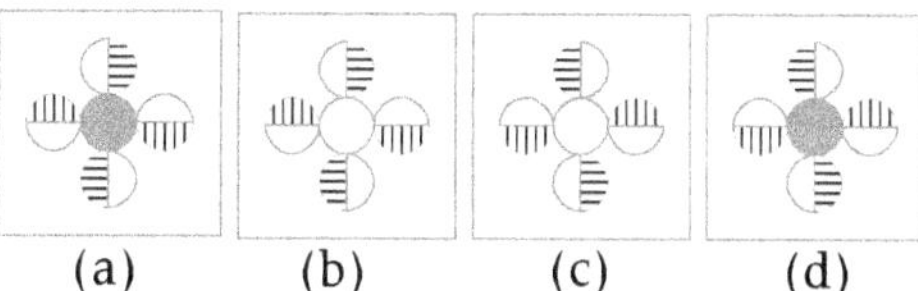

(a) (b) (c) (d)

PRACTICE SET

1 Mark Questions

1. Among M, N, D, P and W, D is taller than M and W. P is taller than D and N. Who among them is shortest?
(a) P (b) D
(c) N (d) Data inadequate

2. How many such 9's are there in the given series each of which immediately followed by an even number and preceded by an odd number?

7 5 6 4 1 9 2 9 8 3 7 5 9 4 6 9 7 9 8 3 5

(a) One (b) Two
(c) Three (d) More than three

3. Choose the correct mirror image of the given word.

JUDGEMENT

(a) TNEMEGDUJ (b) TИƎMƎGDUႱ
(c) TИƎMƎӘDUႱ (d) ႱUDGƎMƎИT

4. Choose the word which completes the second pair in the same way as the first pair.
Painting : Artist : Art gallary :: Pen : ? : ?
(a) Pencil : Bag
(b) Writing : Literature
(c) Diary : Stationery Shop
(d) Colour : Drawing

5. Find the option which contains figure (X) as its part.

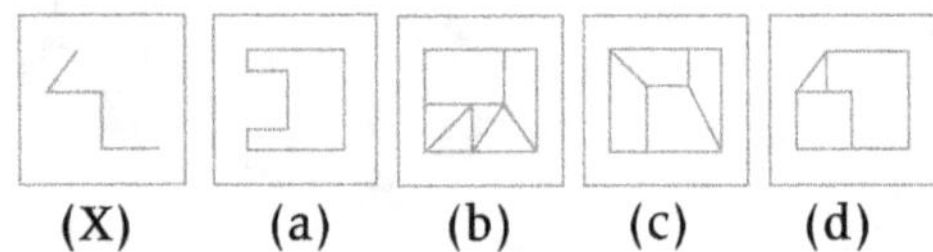

(X) (a) (b) (c) (d)

6. In a certain code language, if 'nice boy honest' is coded as 'eou gou quo' and 'nice state famous' is coded as 'quo you lou', then in the same code 'nice is famous' is coded as?
(a) quo lou pou (b) muo gou lou
(c) quo tuo muo (d) tuo eou quo

7. Find the odd one out.

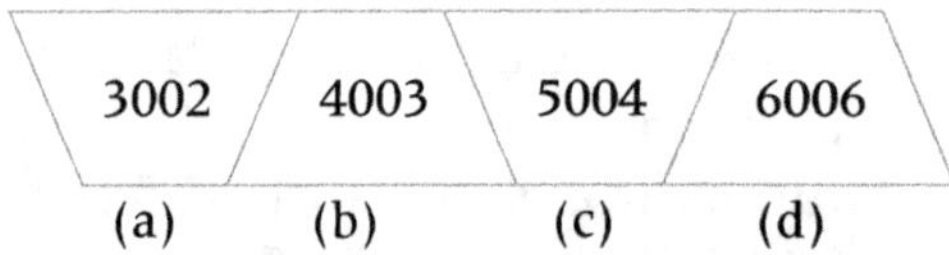

(a) (b) (c) (d)

8. Find the pattern which will appear on the transparent sheet after it is folded along the dotted line.

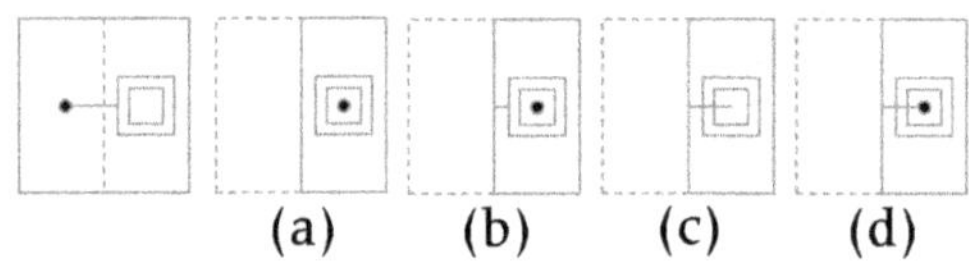

(a) (b) (c) (d)

9. If signs '+' and '–' are interchanged, and number '5' and '8' are interchanged, then which of the following expression is true?
(a) $82 - 35 + 55 = 2$
(b) $82 - 35 + 55 = 102$
(c) $85 - 38 + 85 = 132$
(d) $52 - 35 + 55 = 72$

10. What comes next in the series given below?

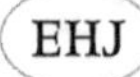

GJI ILH KNG ?

(a) MPF (b) LOH (c) ILF (d) MPI

11. Find the missing number.

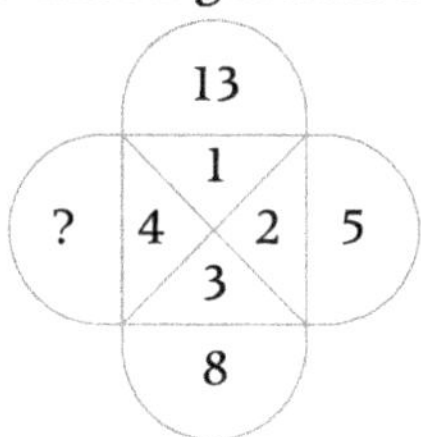

(a) 10 (b) 11 (c) 12 (d) 13

12. P's father is Q's son. M is the paternal uncle of P and N is the brother of Q. How is N related to M?

(a) Brother (b) Nephew
(c) Cousin (d) None of these

13. A watch read 9:30. If the hour hand is in North direction then the minute hand will be in .... direction.

(a) East (b) West
(c) North-East (d) South

14. Choose the correct water image of the given number.

969

(a) 966 (b) 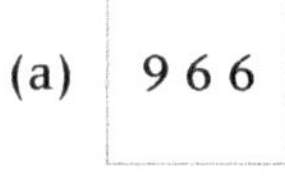

(c) (d)

15. Find the price of 200 shirts, if the price of 40 shirts is given to us as ₹ 1600.

(a) ₹ 4000 (b) ₹ 8000
(c) ₹ 1500 (d) ₹ 1290

16. Find the odd one out.

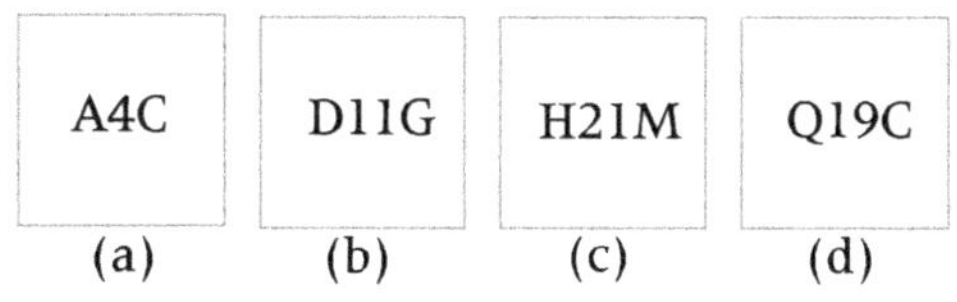

(a) (b) (c) (d)

17. Which figure will complete the second pair in the similar way as first pair?

(a) (b) (c) (d)

18. Choose the correct mirror image of the given figure (X).

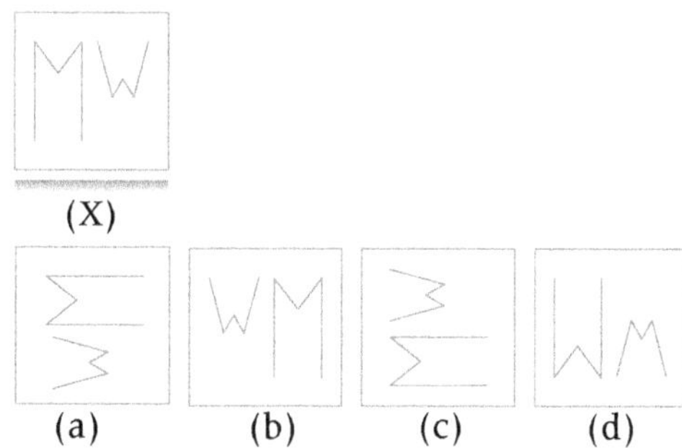

(X)

(a) (b) (c) (d)

19. Choose the correct water image of the given figure (X).

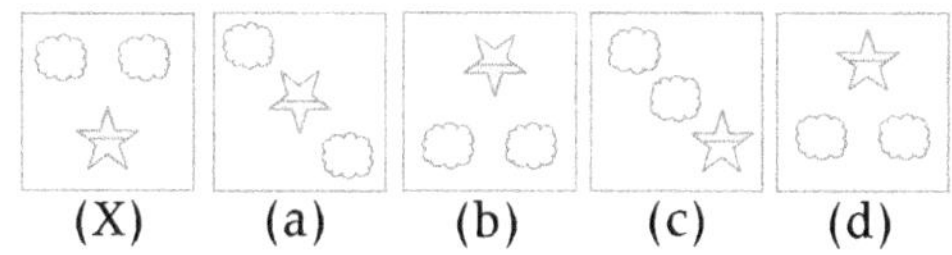

(X) (a) (b) (c) (d)

Directions (Q. Nos. 20 and 21) Read the following information and answer the questions given below it:

A is the father of C. But C is not his son.
E is the daughter of C. F is the spouse of A.
B is the brother of C. D is the son of B.
G is the spouse of B. H is the father of G.

20. Who is the son of F?

(a) B (b) C
(c) D (d) E

21. C is A's father's nephew. D is A's cousin but not the brother of C. How is D related to C?
(a) Father (b) Sister
(c) Mother (d) Aunt

22. Find the missing number.

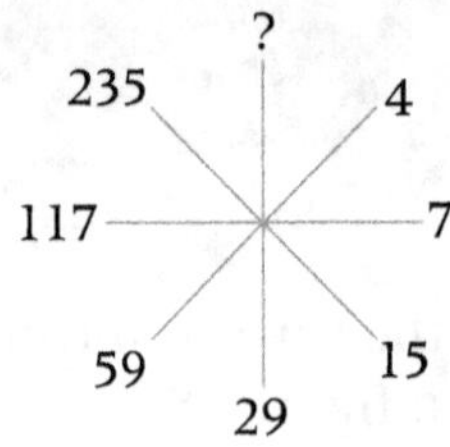

(a) 327 (b) 386
(c) 438 (d) 469

23. Choose the correct pattern that will complete the grid.

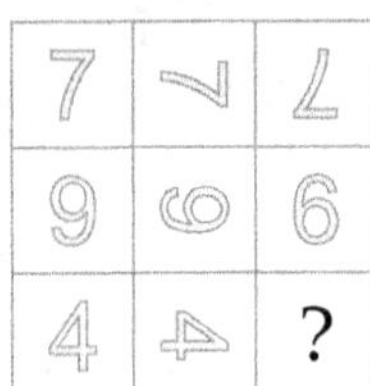

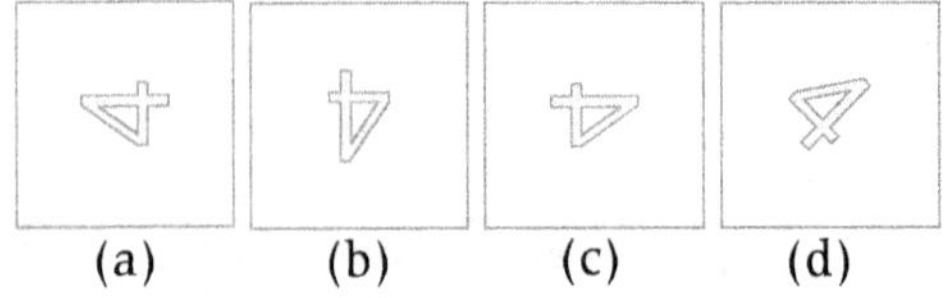

(a) (b) (c) (d)

24. In the following question, arrange the words in a meaningful and logical order and then select the appropriate sequence from the alternatives provided below.
1. Puberty 2. Infancy
3. Adulthood 4. Childhood
5. Senescence
(a) 2, 4, 1, 3, 5 (b) 5, 4, 3, 2, 1
(c) 1, 5, 2, 4, 3 (d) 2, 4, 3, 1, 5

25. Find the pattern which will appear on the transparent sheet after it is folded along the dotted line.

Transparent Sheet

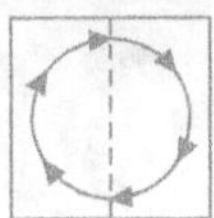

Answer Sheets

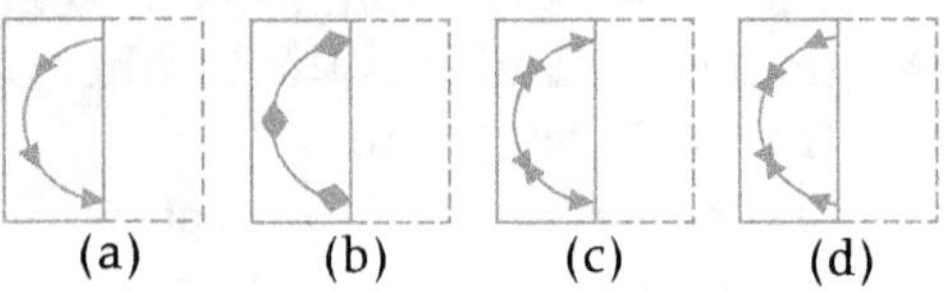

(a) (b) (c) (d)

26. Find the correct figure combination in the given figure matrix.

1	2	3
4	5	6
7	8	9

(a) 1, 5, 7; 2, 6, 9; 3, 4, 8
(b) 1, 2, 3; 4, 5, 6; 7, 8, 9
(c) 1, 6, 9; 5, 7, 8; 3, 4, 2
(d) None of the above

27. Find the missing figure in the series given below:

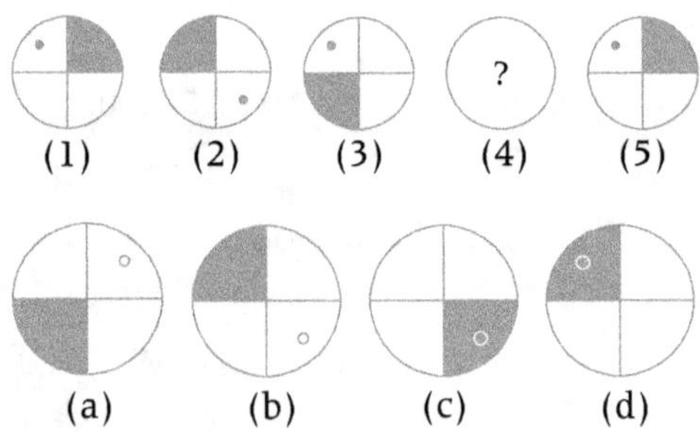

(a) (b) (c) (d)

28. If 'MANGO' can be coded as '273291531', then 'PEA' will be coded as .....

(a) 23173 (b) 33113 (c) 11333 (d) 17332

29. One morning Raju started to walk towards his school. After covering 5 km distance in East, he turned to the left and walk 2 km, then again turns to the right and walk 5 km. He again turns to the left. Now, in which direction is he facing?

(a) East (b) West (c) North (d) South

30. Find the missing number.

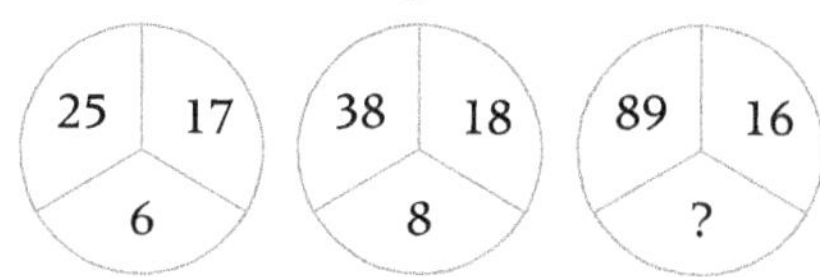

(a) 13 (b) 15 (c) 17 (d) 19

31. Consider the figures (X) and (Y) showing a sheet of paper folded and punched in figure (Z). Select the figure, which will most closely resemble the unfolded form of figure.

Transparent sheets

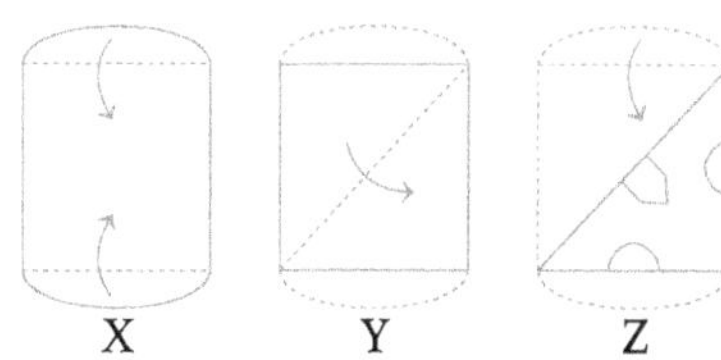

X Y Z

Answer Sheets

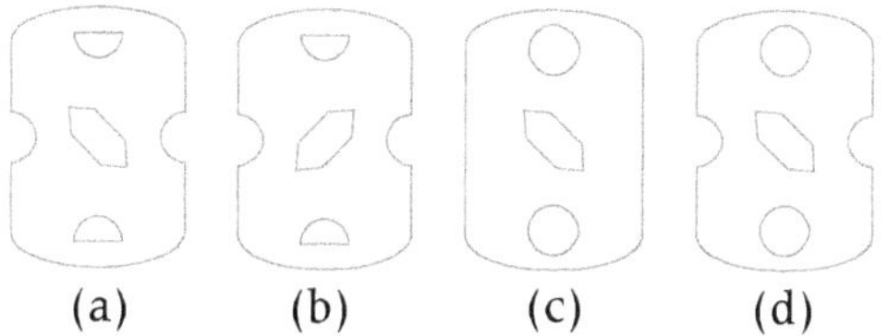

(a) (b) (c) (d)

32. Which of the following word will come second from right end, if all of them are arranged alphabetically as in a dictionary?

(a) Afford (b) Avoid
(c) Answer (d) After

33. Choose the correct mirror image of the given figure (X).

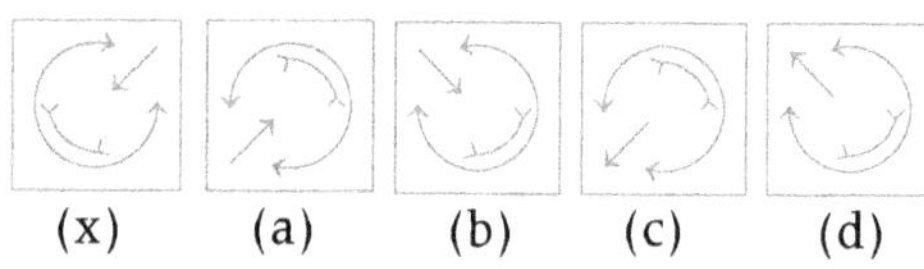

(x) (a) (b) (c) (d)

34. Choose the pair which shows a relation similar to the one expressed in the given pair.

DARE : HEVI

(a) SAID : WENH
(b) JNOP : ORTV
(c) MAIN : QEMR
(d) PLAN : UPHS

35. Find the odd one out.

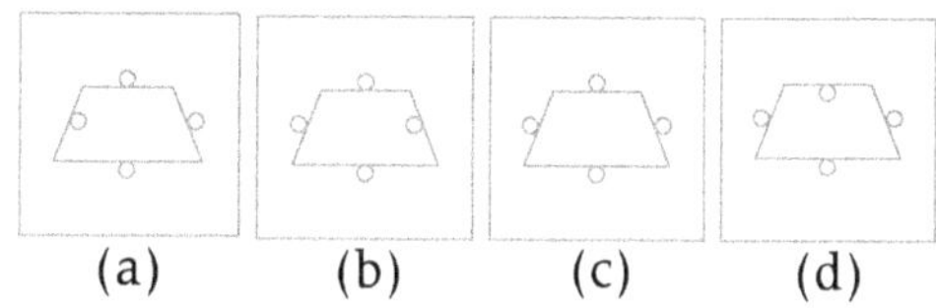

(a) (b) (c) (d)

36. If '@' means divide, '%' means equal to, '#' means add, '*' means greater than, '&' means less than, '>' means multiply and '<' means subtract, then which of the following option is correct?

(a) 10 ÷ 4 # 2 > 6 ÷ 8 > 2
(b) 10 > 4 # 2 & 6 > 8 < 2
(c) 10 # 4 < 2 = 6 < 8 # 2
(d) 10 < 4 # 2 * 6 > 8 # 2

37. Find the missing character.

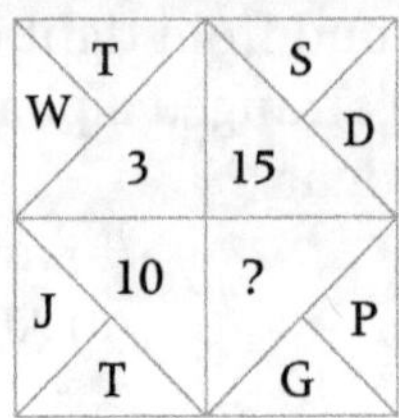

(a) 5 (b) 9 (c) 11 (d) 13

38. In a row of 40 boys facing North. Amar is 6th to the right of Sudeep and Sudeep is 11th to the left of Aman. If Amar is 28th from the right end of the row. What is the position of Aman from the left end of the row?

(a) 21th (b) 20th (c) 17th (d) 18th

39. In the given sequence of letters, how many C's are followed by D's but not preceded by E's?

E C D C E C D E E C D E D D C D E C E D C E

(a) One (b) Two
(c) Three (d) None

40. Consider the figures (X) and (Y) showing a sheet of paper folded and punched in figure (Z). Select the figure, which will most closely resemble the unfolded form of figure.

Transparent Sheets

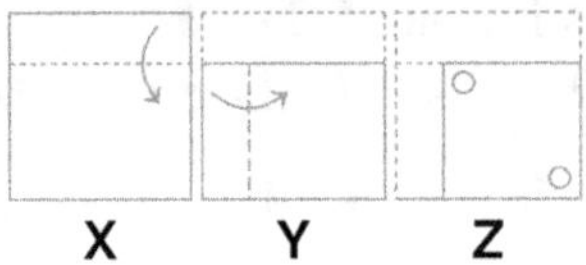

Answer Sheets

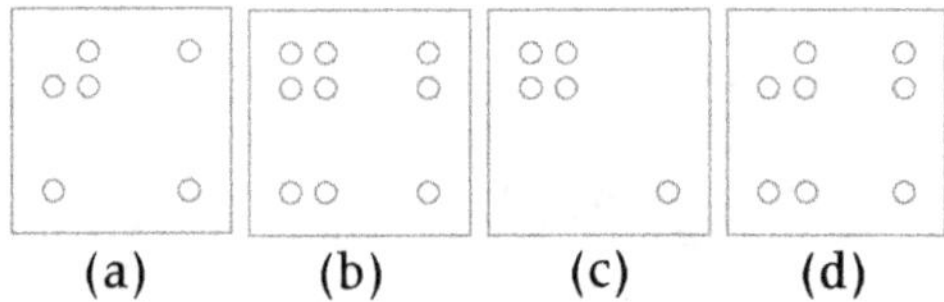

2 Marks Questions

Directions (Q. Nos. 41 and 42) Study the following information and answers the given questions.

(i) B and E are good in Dramatics and Computer Science.
(ii) A and B are good in Computer Science and Physics.
(iii) A, D and C are good in Physics and History.
(iv) C and A are good in Physics and Mathematics.
(v) D and E are good in History and Dramatics?

41. Who is good in Physics, History and Dramatics?

(a) A (b) B (c) D (d) E

42. Who is good in Physics, History and Mathematics, but not in Computer Science?

(a) A (b) B
(c) C (d) D

43. Sonia left for her college by car. She drove 16 km towards North and then 12 km towards West. Then, she turned to the South and covered 6 km. Further, she turned to the East and moved 10 km. Finally, she turned right and drove 10 km. How far and in which direction is she from her starting point?

(a) 4 km, West (b) 4 km, East
(c) 2 km, West (d) 2 km, East

44. Akshay is 16th from the left end in the row of boys and Vijay is 18th from the right end. Avinash is 11th from Akshay toward to right end and 3rd from Vijay towards the right end. How many boys are there in the row?

(a) 41 (b) 40
(c) 39 (d) 38

Directions (Q. Nos. 45 and 46) The table given below gives the code for some letters in the form of symbol. Answer the following questions based on the table.

Letters	Z	D	M	T	J	P	V	N	E	U	Q	I
Symbols	+	@	β	<	&	d	=	*	γ	#	>	[]

45. The word which is coded as β&γ #+ >* is....

(a) MPEZINJ
(b) MJEUZQN
(c) MJUEQZN
(d) MEJUZQN

46. The code for the word TNUDQ is

(a) <*@#* (b) @#>*<
(c) *@<#> (d) <*#@>

47. Select the figure from the options which will continue the same series as extablished by the problem figures.

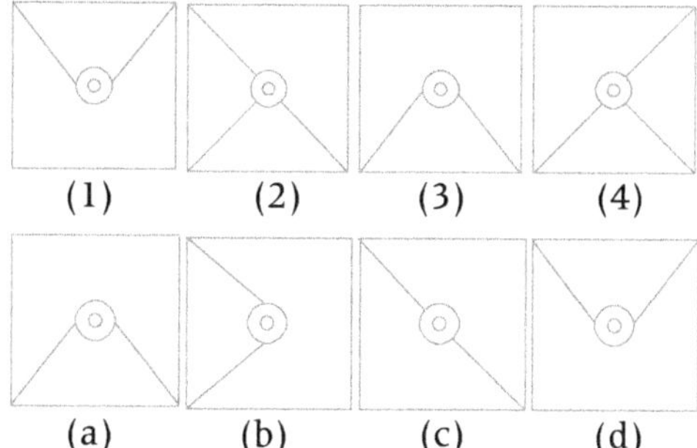

48. Determine the missing term.

AE : 36 CD : 49 EF : ?

(a) 196 (b) 2 (c) 11 (d) 121

49. If 'LM' stands for '+', 'MN' stands for '–', 'No' stands for '×' and 'OP' stands for '÷', then what is the value of 14NO10LM42OP2MN6?

(a) 155 (b) 248 (c) 250 (d) 216

50. Which of the following option figure would complete the pattern given in figure (X)?

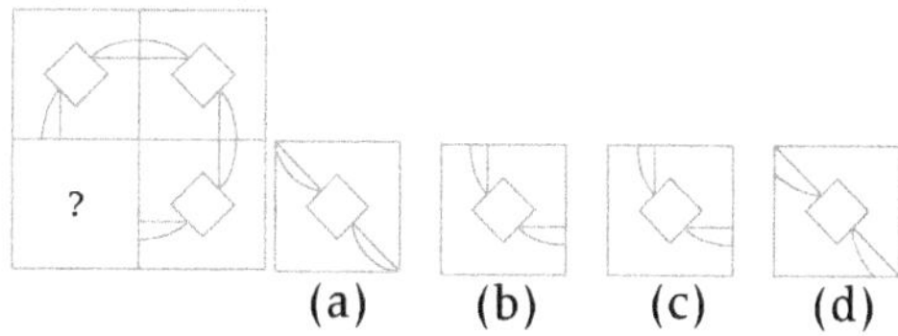

Hints & Solutions

1. Matching Pairs

1. *(d)* As, $186 \Rightarrow 18/6 = 3$
   Similarly, $6513 = 65/13 = \boxed{5}$
   We can see first two digits of the given number are divided by the third one.

2. *(c)* As, $4 \times 2 = 8$ and $8 + 1 = 9$
   Similarly, $7 \times 2 = 14$
   and $14 + 1 = \boxed{15}$
   Hence, option (c) is correct

3. *(c)* As, $6248 / 2 = 3124$
   Similarly, $4024 / 2 = \boxed{2012}$
   Hence, option (c) is correct.

4. *(b)* As, $423539 - 1000 = 422539$
   Similarly, $253682 - 1000 = 252682$
   Hence, option (b) is correct.

5. *(c)* As, $X \xrightarrow{+2} Z$, $W \xrightarrow{+2} Y$
   Similary, $D \xrightarrow{+2} \boxed{F}$, $J \xrightarrow{+2} \boxed{L}$
   Hence, option (c) is correct.

6. *(a)* As, $A \xrightarrow{+1} B$ Similarly, $\boxed{L} \xrightarrow{+1} M$
   $B \xrightarrow{+2} D$ $\boxed{M} \xrightarrow{+2} O$
   $C \xrightarrow{+3} F$ $\boxed{J} \xrightarrow{+3} M$
   Hence, option (a) is correct.

7. *(a)* Here, in first pair, the letters in first group are reversed to obtain the second group of letters. Similarly, reversing the letters HIJ, we get JIH.
   Hence, option (a) is correct.

8. *(b)* As, P N G R S
   (+2) (+2) (+2)
   R R I N U
   Similarly, G P D C M
   (+2) (+2) (+2)
   $\boxed{\text{I C F P O}}$
   Hence, option (b) is correct.

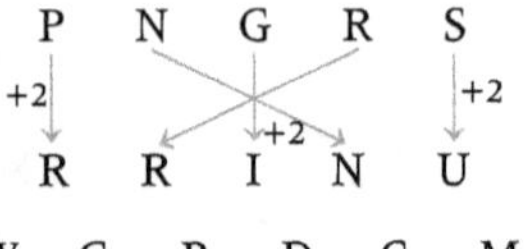

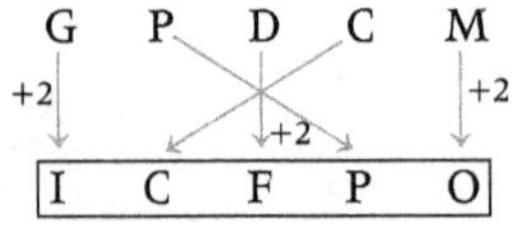

9. *(b)* As, a helicopter is a type of an aircraft. Similarly, an almond is a type of a nut.
   Hence, option (b) is correct.

10. *(c)* Peacock is the national bird of India. In the same way, Kangaroo is the national animal of Australia.
    Hence, option (c) is correct.

11. *(c)* A car is a type of an automobile. Similarly, a cat is a type of an animal.
    Hence, option (c) is correct.

12. *(b)* As, a mother is a parent, in the same way a sister is a sibling.
    Hence, option (b) is correct.

13. *(b)* Here, is first pair the dots change their position from left slant to right slant and the black dots become white. On following this pattern, figure (b) will complete the second pair. Hence, option (b) is correct.

14. *(c)* In first pair, both the shapes are laterally inverted and joined together. On following this pattern, figure (c) will complete the second pair.
    Hence, option (c) is correct.

15. *(d)* The positional values of 'G' and 'M' in the English alphabetical series are 7 and 13, respectively. Thus, the given pair has been formed using these positional values. The only pair amongst the four given alternatives, which shows a similar relationship is (P*T : 16*20).
    Hence, option (d) is correct.

16. *(b)* Here, the positional values of the letters in English alphabets are added to obtain the number.
    As, B = 2, D = 4 and 2 + 4 = 6
    Similarly, L = 12, K = 11 and $12 + 11 = \boxed{23}$
    Hence, option (b) is correct.

17. *(b)* In each pair, digits of the first number are reversed to obtain the second number. On reversing the digits of 929, we get 929.
    Hence, option (b) is correct.

18. *(c)* As, $C \xrightarrow{+5} H$
    $A \xrightarrow{+5} F$
    $R \xrightarrow{+5} W$
    $E \xrightarrow{+5} J$

Similarly, in option (c), $G \xrightarrow{+5} L$, $O \xrightarrow{+5} T$, $A \xrightarrow{+5} F$, $L \xrightarrow{+5} Q$ → LTFQ

Hence, option (c) is correct.

19. *(c)* As, $G \longleftrightarrow T-1=S$

$R \longleftrightarrow I-1=H$

$E \longleftrightarrow V-1=U$

$A \longleftrightarrow Z-1=Y$

$T \longleftrightarrow G-1=F$

Letters at the same position in backward alphabetical series

Similarly, $W \longleftrightarrow D-1=$ C

$O \longleftrightarrow L-1=$ K

$R \longleftrightarrow I-1=$ H

$L \longleftrightarrow O-1=$ N

$D \longleftrightarrow W-1=$ V

Hence, option (c) is the correct answer.

20. *(a)* In each pair, the positional values of the letters are added to give the number.

As, $A=1, B=2$

$1+2=3$

and $C=3, D=4$

$3+4=7$

Similarly, $E=5, F=6$

$5+6=\boxed{11}$

Hence, option (a) is correct.

21. *(a)* As, first figure is divided into eight parts so, $(8)^3=512$

Similarly, second figure is divided into six parts so, $(6)^3=\boxed{216}$

Hence, option (a) is correct.

22. *(b)* As, $S \Rightarrow 19$

$\Rightarrow \quad 19+(19+1)=19+20=39$ and $M \Rightarrow 13$

$\Rightarrow 13+(13+1)=13+14=27$

Similarly, $Y \Rightarrow 25$

$\Rightarrow 25+(25+1)=25+26=\boxed{51}$

Henc, option (b) is correct.

23. *(c)* As, in first figure there are two triangles. So, $(2)^2=4$ and 4 is the place value of D and the reverse place value of D is W.

So, we get $(2)^2=4 \rightarrow D \leftrightarrow W$

Similarly, in the second figure there are 3 squares. So, $(3)^2=9$ and 9 is the place value of I and the reverse place value of I is R.

So, we get, $(3)^2=9 \rightarrow I \leftrightarrow \boxed{R}$

Hence, option (c) is correct.

2. Odd One Out

1. *(c)* In each group of letters except DG, one letter is skipped in between the two letters.

So, DG is the odd one.

Hence, option (c) is correct.

2. *(d)* In each group of letters except DON, the letters when read from backward (i.e., the right end) form a group of three consecutive letters.

Hence, option (d) is correct..

3. *(a)* All the group of letters except CDWX, have atleast one vowel, while group CDWX does not have any vowel.

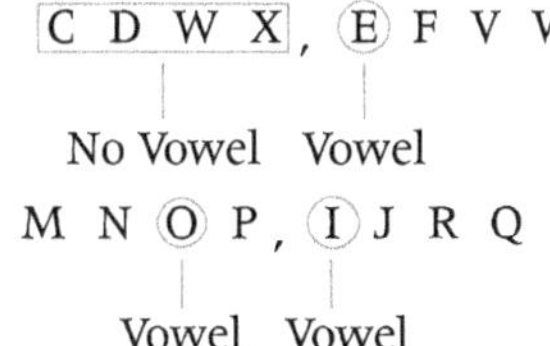

Hence, option (a) is correct.

4. *(c)* Except 99, all others are perfect squares. So, 99 is odd one.

Hence, option (c) is correct.

5. *(b)* Except option (b), all others are multiples of 7. Hence, option (b) is odd one.

6. *(c)* 34<u>5</u>, 36<u>5</u>, 380, 30<u>5</u>

Here, every number except 380 has 5 at its unit's place. Hence, option (c) is odd one.

7. *(b)* Except Lungs, all others are external body argans. Hence, option (b) is correct.

8. *(d)* All except Beijing are countries. Beijing is the capital of People's Republic of China. Hence, option (d) is correct.

9. *(c)* A bicycle is moved by pedals while all others vehicles runs on fuel.

Hence, option (c) is correct.

10. *(c)* Except option (c), in all the three figures have two squares, one circle and one triangle while in figure (c) there are two circles, one

triangle and one square.
Hence, option (c) is correct.

11. *(b)* Except figure (b), all other figures have same number of black dots as that of number of lines. But in figure (b) the number of lines is 6 and black dots are 8. So, figure (b) is odd one. Hence, option (b) is correct.

12. *(d)* Except option (d), the numerical value along with the letters is the reverse place value of that letter. But in option (d), the reverse place value of G is 20 not 26. So, option (d) is odd.

    Hence, option (d) is correct.

13. *(b)* Except option (b), there are two letters present with a geometrical figure but in option (b) there are three letters so option (b) is odd. Hence, option (b) is correct.

14. *(d)* In all the figures, except figure (d), the arrows are moving in anti-clockwise direction. But in figure (d) the arrows are moving in clockwise direction. So, figure (d) is odd one. Hence, option (d) is correct.

15. *(d)* In all the figures except figure (d), the bent line and pin are on opposite sides of the object. But in figure (d) both are on same side. So, figure (d) is odd one.
    Hence, option (d) is correct.

16. *(b)* Except option (b), numerical value is the (total number of letter + 2) letters present in the word but in option (b) 'MAN' has three letters. So the sum should be '3 + 2 = 5' but here '7' is given. So, option (b) is odd.

    Hence option (b) is correct.

17. *(c)* All except 'KLOP' have a difference of two positions between the second and third letter.

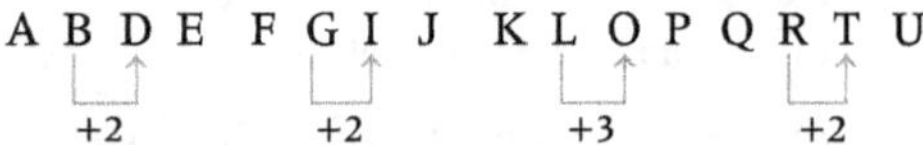

∴ KLOP is the odd one.

18. *(b)* All except 'IJKL' have two small and two capital letters.

19. *(d)* All except 'KEAR' are meaningful words.

20. *(c)* All except '18, 36, 40' have second number double the first number and third number is 6 more than the second number.

21. *(b)* RARCTO ⇒ CARROT

    NIATCRU ⇒ CURTAIN

    BACGEBA ⇒ CABBAGE

    ILBJARN ⇒ BRINJAL

    All except 'Curtain' are vegetables.

3. What Comes Next?

1. *(b)* The pattern is as follows

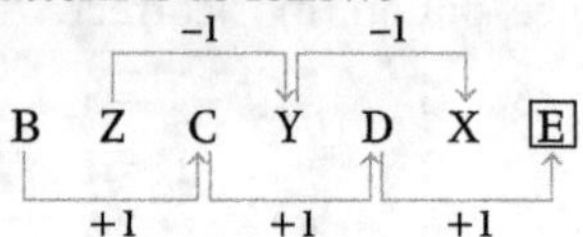

Therefore, next letter will be E.

Hence, option (b) is correct.

2. *(d)* The pattern is as follows

A $\xrightarrow{+2}$ C $\xrightarrow{+3}$ F $\xrightarrow{+4}$ J $\xrightarrow{+5}$ O

B $\xrightarrow{+3}$ E $\xrightarrow{+4}$ I $\xrightarrow{+5}$ N $\xrightarrow{+6}$ T

Hence, option (d) is correct.

3. *(b)* The pattern is as follows

+3 +3 +3 +3

AC DF GI JL MO

+3 +3 +3 +3

Hence, option (b) is correct.

4. *(c)* The pattern is as follows

B $\xrightarrow{+0}$ B $\xrightarrow{+1}$ C $\xrightarrow{+2}$ E $\xrightarrow{+3}$ H $\xrightarrow{+4}$ L $\xrightarrow{+5}$ Q

A $\xrightarrow{+0}$ A $\xrightarrow{+1}$ B $\xrightarrow{+2}$ D $\xrightarrow{+3}$ G $\xrightarrow{+4}$ K $\xrightarrow{+5}$ P

Hence, option (c) is correct.

5. *(c)* The middle letters are static. So, lets concentrate on the first and third letter.

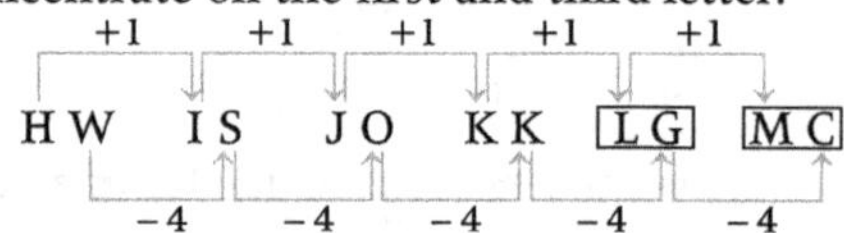

Hence, option (c) is correct.

6. *(d)* The pattern is as follows:

98 $\xrightarrow{-8}$ 90 $\xrightarrow{-8}$ 82 $\xrightarrow{-8}$ 74 $\xrightarrow{-8}$ 66

Hence, option (d) is correct.

7. *(a)* The pattern is as follows

400 $\xrightarrow{\div 2}$ 200 $\xrightarrow{\div 2}$ 100 $\xrightarrow{\div 2}$ 50 $\xrightarrow{\div 2}$ 25

Hence, option (a) is correct.

8. *(b)* The pattern is as follows

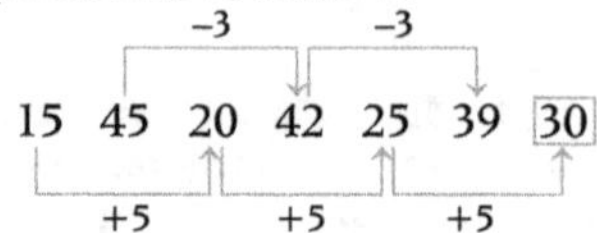

Hence, option (b) is correct.

9. *(c)* The pattern is as follows

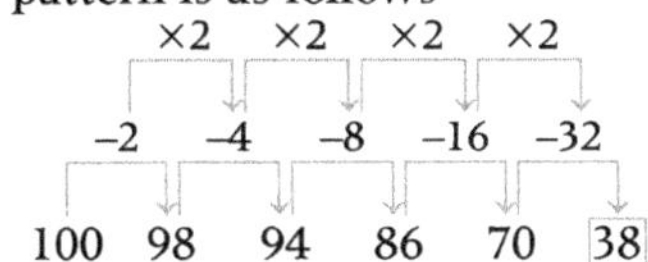

Hence, option (c) is correct.

10. *(c)* The pattern is as follows

8 66 8   9 56 6   7 37 5

As, $8 \times 8 + 2 = 66$, $9 \times 6 + 2 = 56$

Similarly, $7 \times 5 + 2 = 37$

Hence, option (c) is correct.

11. *(d)* The pattern is as follows

$2004 \xrightarrow{+5} 2009 \xrightarrow{+7} 2016 \xrightarrow{+9} 2025 \xrightarrow{+11} 2036 \xrightarrow{+13} 2049 \xrightarrow{+15} 2064$

Hence, option (d) is correct.

12. *(b)* Here, a square is removed from the line in each successive step moving in anti-clockwise direction. On following this pattern, option figure (b) will complete the series.

Hence, option (b) is correct.

13. *(a)* Option figure (a) will complete the series.

14. *(a)* Here, in each step the number of stair is increasing by one. On following this pattern, option figure (a) will complete the series.

Hence, option (a) is correct.

15. *(b)* Here, square is moving anti-clockwise from one corner to another and dot is moving clockwise from one corner to another.

On following this pattern, the next two figures are shown as below

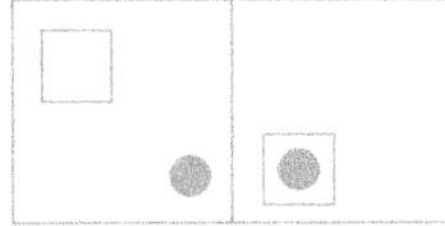

Hence, option (b) is correct.

16. *(b)* Option figure (b) will complete the series.

Hence, option (b) is correct.

17. *(b)* In the given series, addition of numbers in each term gives the place value of letter.

The pattern is as follow

$0 + 1 \longrightarrow 1$, place value of A

$1 + 1 \longrightarrow 2$, place value of B

$2 + 1 \longrightarrow 3$, place value of C

$2 + 2 \longrightarrow 4$, place value of D

$2 + 3 \longrightarrow 5$, place value of E

$3 + 3 \longrightarrow 6$, place value of F

$3 + 4 \longrightarrow 7$, place value of G

So, letter in next term will be G and place value of G is 7.

18. *(d)* The pattern is as follows

A → A → A → A → A → A

$B \xrightarrow{+1} C \xrightarrow{+1} D \xrightarrow{+1} E \xrightarrow{+1} F \xrightarrow{+1} G$

9	16	25	36	49	64
↓	↓	↓	↓	↓	↓
3^2	4^2	5^2	6^2	7^2	8^2

Hence, option (d) is correct.

19. *(b)* Here we can see that the II and IV letter is static. The first and third consist an alphabetic order beginning with letter 'D'.

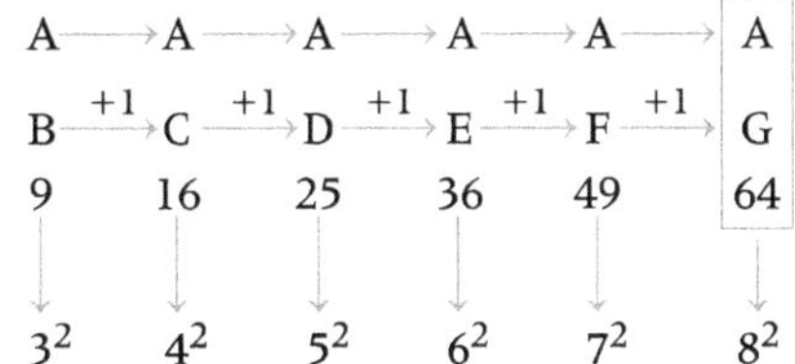

So, we get 'LXMM'.

Hence, option (b) is correct.

20. *(b)* The pattern is as follows, the number $\times \frac{1}{2}$.

So, the missing number is

$12 \times \frac{1}{2} = 6 \Rightarrow 6 \times \frac{1}{2} = 3$

$\Rightarrow 3 \times \frac{1}{2} = \frac{3}{2} = 1\frac{1}{2} \Rightarrow \frac{3}{2} \times \frac{1}{2} = \frac{3}{4} \Rightarrow \frac{3}{4} \times \frac{1}{2} = \frac{3}{8}$

Hence, option (b) is correct.

21. *(b)* Here, in every group, each letter is rotating 90° in clockwise direction.

On following this pattern, option figure (b) will complete the series.

Hence, option (b) is correct.

22. *(d)* In first step, the lowermost zig-zag line is converted into a triangle. In second step, the lowermost line converted into circle and second lowermost line converted into triangle in the same way in the third step, second lower most line converted into circle and third.

Hence, option (d) is correct.

23. *(a)* The pattern is as follows

$A \xrightarrow{+3} D \xrightarrow{+3} G \xrightarrow{+3} J \xrightarrow{+3} M \xrightarrow{+3} \boxed{P}$

$2 \xrightarrow{+3} 5 \xrightarrow{+3} 8 \xrightarrow{+3} 11 \xrightarrow{+3} 14 \xrightarrow{+3} \boxed{17}$

$C \xrightarrow{+3} F \xrightarrow{+3} I \xrightarrow{+3} L \xrightarrow{+3} O \xrightarrow{+3} \boxed{R}$

Hence, option (a) is correct.

4. Coding-Decoding

1. *(d)* As,

H	E	A	L	T	H
−1 ↓	−1 ↓	−1 ↓	−1 ↓	−1 ↓	−1 ↓
G	D	Z	K	S	G

Similarly,

N	O	R	T	H
−1 ↓	−1 ↓	−1 ↓	−1 ↓	−1 ↓
M	N	Q	S	G

Hence, option (d) is correct.

2. *(a)* As,

C	O	R	D	I	A	L
+2 ↓	−1 ↓	+2 ↓	−1 ↓	+2 ↓	−1 ↓	+2 ↓
E	N	T	C	K	Z	N

Similarly,

S	O	M	E	D	A	Y
+2 ↓	−1 ↓	+2 ↓	−1 ↓	+2 ↓	−1 ↓	+2 ↓
U	N	O	D	F	Z	A

Hence, option (a) is correct.

3. *(b)* As,

M	O	C	K	S
+1 ↓	−1 ↓	+1 ↓	−1 ↓	+1 ↓
N	N	D	J	T

Similarly,

F	L	A	M	E
+1 ↓	−1 ↓	+1 ↓	−1 ↓	+1 ↓
G	K	B	L	F

4. *(b)* Here, letters are coded by numbers as

From BAKE, we get

$B \to 5$, $A \to 7$, $K \to 9$, $E \to 6$

From FIRE, we get

$F \to 3$, $I \to 1$, $R \to 4$, $E \to 6$

Therefore, FEAR $\to \boxed{3674}$

Hence, option (b) is correct.

5. *(a)* Here, each letter is coded by its position in English alphabetical order

MORNS → 1315181419

6. *(c)* Here, letter's positional value × 2

i.e, $A \to 1 \times 2 = 2$, $D \to 4 \times 2 = 8$,

$K \to 11 \times 2 = 22$,

and T E N
↓ ↓ ↓
$40 + 10 + 28 = 78$

Therefore, $B = 2 \times 2 \to 4$

$E = 5 \times 2 \to 10$,

$L = 12 \times 2 \to 24$

So, code for BEL is $4 + 10 + 24 = \boxed{38}$

Hence, option (c) is correct.

7. *(a)* Clearly, we can see that each word is coded by numeral which is 1 less than the number is written at the ten's place of the letters in the word and this numeral.

Since, there are '9' letters in the word 'CHALLENGE' so, required code $= 9 - 1 = 8$

and this numeral is converted into its ten's value i.e, '80'. Hence, option (a) is correct.

8. *(a)* Here each letter is coded as twice its position in reverse English alphabetical order as

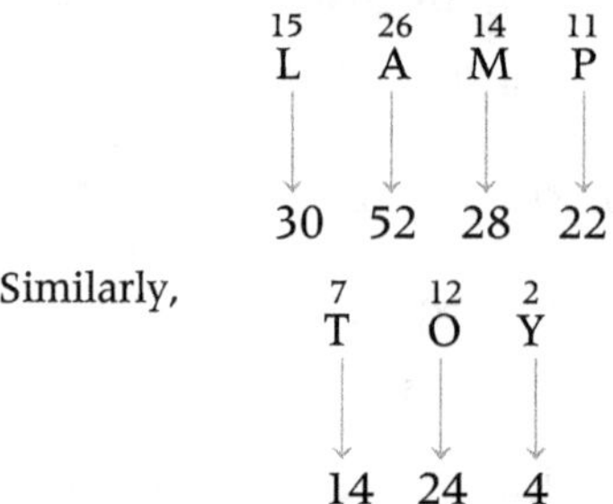

9. *(c)* We know that, colour of milk is white. But in the given code white is coded as blue.

So, the colour of milk is blue.

Hence, option (c) is correct.

10. *(c)* We know that fruits grow on 'tree' and here 'tree' is called 'sky'.So, the fruits grow on the 'sky'.

Hence, option (c) is correct.

11. *(c)* According to the question,

△2 ⑤ □6 → You □are ◯good ...(i)

□6 △3 7 → we □are △bad ...(ii)

△3 ⑤ 8 → ◯good and △bad ...(iii)

It is clear that, in Eqs. (i) and (iii) the common digit is 5 and the common word is 'good'.

In Eqs. (ii) and (iii) the common code digit is 3 and the common word is 'bad'.

So, '5' means 'good' and '3' means 'bad'.

Therefore, from the Eq. (iii) 'and' means '8'.

Hence, option (c) is correct.

12. *(b)* According to the question,

si# po@ re$ → effort is good ...(i)

ti# na@ re$ → real is time ...(ii)

ka* si# → interesting effort ...(iii)

de$ ti# → that real ...(iv)

It is clear from (i), (ii) and (iii).

that ⇒ de$; is ⇒ re$

effort => Si#

∴'that is effort' will be coded as 'de$ re$si#.

Hence option (b) is correct.

13. ho na ta → food is good ...(i)

Sa ta la → eat food regularly ...(ii)

da na ja → keep good health ...(iii)

From Eqs. (i) and (ii), 'food' is common in both (i) and (ii) and code 'ta' is also common in both (i) and (ii). So, code for 'food' is 'ta'.

Hence, option (b) is correct.

14. *(a)* Letters are coded by symbols as

Letters	R	A	I	D	P	E
Symbols	%	#	©	$	@	★

Therefore, DEAR is coded as $★ #%.

Hence, option (a) is correct.

15. *(b)* In the word 'SOLUTION' the vowels O, U and I are in the middle. So, each of these will be coded as 3 by the condition (ii). Therefore, the code for 'SOLUTION' will be '53238331'.

Hence, option (b) is correct.

16. *(c)* In the word 'ENCOURAGE' the first and last place have the same vowel 'E'. So, by the condition (iv) 'E' will be coded as '@'. The vowel A, O and U are in the middle. So, by the condition (ii) these will be coded as '3'.

Therefore, the code for the 'ENCOURAGE' will be '@1733536@'.

Hence, the option (c) is correct.

Sol. (Q. Nos. 17 and 18) The given information can be represented as

plot for all persons → fn bo dl sw ...(i)

find the hidden plot → dl et ga nu ...(ii)

try and find out → ga yc mp zh ...(iii)

for the lock out → nu mp fn rv ...(iv)

From Eqs. (i), (ii), (iii) and (iv), we get

Persons = bo/sw, try = yc/zh

17. *(c)* 'try the key' → 'nu ka yc'

∴ try = yc and key = ka

Hence, key and lock → ka zh rv

18. *(b)* 'sw' stands for either 'persons' or 'all'.

5. Alphabet and Number Test

1. *(c)* As it can be seen from the table

A B C D E F G H I J K L M N O P Q R S T U V W X Y Z

← 6th to the left

the position of 'O' is '15th'. Sixth to left of 'O' means (15–6). i.e, 9th position. Clearly, the letter 'I' is present at 9th position. Hence, option (c) is correct.

2. *(b)* As it can be seen from the table

The 14th letter from the right is 'M' and 9th letter to the left of 'M' is 'D'. Hence, option (b) is correct.

3. *(b)* As it can be seen from the table below

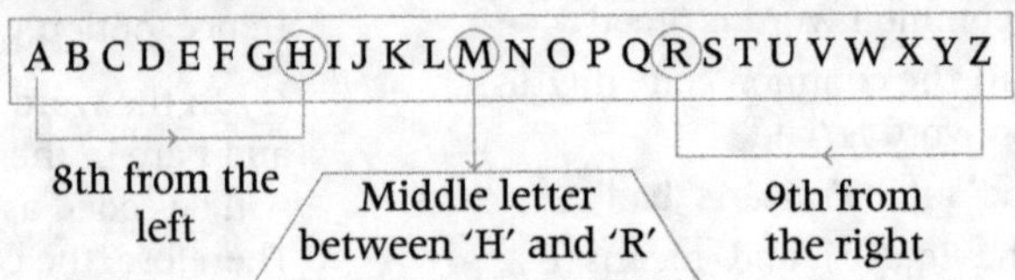

8th letter from the left = H, 9th letter from the right = R.So, the middle letter between the letters 'H' and 'R' will be 'M'.
Hence, option (b) is correct.

4. *(c)* As per the question, the letters are arranged in reverse order as shown below

from left ←——16——→
ZYX W VUTSRQPONML K JIHGFEDCBA
←——12——→ To right

It is clear that, W is at 12th position from left of the sixteenth letter from left end.
Hence, option (c) is correct.

5. *(a)* ZYXWVUTSRQPON M LKJIHGFEDCBA
13th from the right end

From the above series, we can see that the thirteenth letter to the right end is M.
Hence, option (a) is correct.

6. *(b)* Clearly, the given letters when arranged in the order of 4, 2, 1, 6, 5, 3, form a word 'HANDLE'. Hence, option (b) is correct.

7. *(b)* By using the letters of the given word 'MEASURE' we can form 'SAME' word.
Hence, option (b) is correct.

8. *(b)* By using the letters of given word 'CORRESPONDING', 'DISCERN' is the only word which can be formed. Hence, option (b) is correct.

9. *(c)* In the given word there is only one 'R' letter and 'E' letter so, 'RETIRE' word cannot be formed.
Hence, option (c) is correct.

10. *(d)* From the given word 'FORM' is the only word which cannot be formed due to the absence of letter 'M'. Hence, option (d) is correct.

11. *(a)* Given word → C A T E G O R Y
After arranging in alphabetical order → A C E G O R T Y
Clearly, only 'Y' remains its same position.
Hence, option (a) is correct.

12. *(b)* The logical sequence of the words are
Seed, Plant, Tree, Wood, Table
i.e. 5 4 3 2 1
Hence, option (b) is correct.

13. *(d)* The logical sequence of the words are
Tree, Branch, Leaves, Flower, Fruit
i.e. 4 2 1 3 5
Hence, option (d) is correct.

14. *(d)* The dictionary sequence of the words are War, Wasp, Waste, Wrist It is clear that,
war comes first.
Hence, option (d) is correct.

15. *(d)* 'R' is fourth from the left end. Hence, option (d) is correct.

16. *(c)* There are 'two' T's which are preceded and followed by Q i.e.,
QTQ TTQ QTQ TTQQQTTQQTTQ QQT.
Hence, option (c) is correct.

17. *(a)* 8 976 3428 976 4592 9 7
From the given number sequence, it is clear that there are two 7's which are preceded by 9 and followed by 6.
Hence, option (a) is correct.

18. *(d)* 89 76342 89 76459 29 7
There are three 9's which are preceded by even numbers.
Hence, option (d) is correct.

19. *(a)* Only one meaningful word is formed by using each letter once i.e., 'REST'.
Hence, option (a) is correct.

20. *(b)* On interchanging the positions of alphabets we get,

PAM UPQ FTS MJS

Clearly , word UPQ Starts with vowel.
Hence, option (b) is correct.

21. *(b)* There are two vowels preceded by a symbol i.e.,

&E and #U

Hence, option (b) is correct.

22. *(c)* On interchanging the positions of digits we get,

913, 904, 814, 917

It is clear that, 418 is the least number.
Hence, option (c) is correct.

23. *(c)*

Given number →	9	8	4	6	6	7	3	2	5
After arranging in descending order →	9	8	7	6	6	5	4	3	2

Clearly, three digits remains its original position i.e, 9, 8 and 6. Hence, option (c) is correct.

6. Raking Test

1. *(b)* Total number of students = (Position from the top) + (Position from the bottom) – Sohan itself = 7 + 26 –1 = 32
Hence, option (b) is correct.

2. (b) Rohit obtained more marks than Tarun, but less than Kabir. i.e. Kabir > Rohit > Tarun.
Raj obtained more than Vansh, but less than Harshit i.e., Harshit > Raj > Vansh.
Now, Kabir obtained less than Vansh i.e.,
Harshit > Raj > Vansh > Kabir > Rohit> Tarun.
So, harshit obtained highest marks.

3. *(c)* According to the question,
Mohit > Rajesh/Raman ...(i)
Raman > Rajeev > Namit > Rajesh ...(ii)
From Eqs. (i) and (ii), we get
Mohit > Raman > Rajeev > Namit > Rajesh
So, Mohit is the oldest among them.

4. *(c)* According to the question,
Number of boys in the row = 6 + 10 + 8 =24
So, there are 24 boys in the row.

5. *(a)* According to the question,
Tripti's new position is 15th from the left. But this is the same as Tusha's earlier position which is 9th from the right.
So, total number of girls =15 + 9 – 1
=24 – 1 =23

6. *(b)* According to the question,
Total number of girls now = (7 + 28) – 1 = 34
So, extra girls need =50 – 34 =16

7. *(a)* According to the question, there will be no change in the ranking list from the top, if we are adding students to the bottom list.
So, Sameer rank is 14th.

8. *(b)* According to the question,
Number of mangoes trees = 6 + 6 –1 =11

9. *(a)* According to the question,
Total number of boys in the line
=15 + 4 – 1 =18
So, number of boys to be added
= 30 – 18 =12

10. *(d)* According to the question,
Number of students = 23 + 36 –1 = 58

11. *(b)* After shifting two places towards left Rohan become 7th from the left end, it means Rohan's earlier position from the left end
= 7 + 2 = 9th
So, Rohan's earlier position from the right end =10 – 9 + 1 = 2nd

12. *(d)* As per ranking of Y and X and the presence of 6 letters between them, the total number of letters in the row will be
= 6 +18 + 6= 30
Now, we can see that it is already a group of 30 letters. Hence, no more letters are required to be added to the group.

13. *(d)* According to the question,
Miransh new position is 15th from the right as well as the left end of the row.
So, number of students in the queue
=14 +1 + 14 = 29

14. (b)

Anni Shubh
Left end ——— Right end
19th
20th

There are 6 boys between Anni and Shubh.
Anni's position from left end = 20 − 7 = 13
So, total number of boys in the line
= 13 + 19 − 1 = 31
(13: Anni's position from left end; 19: Anni's position from right end)

15. (c) Given, total number of persons in the queue = 50

Number of persons between Sarthak and Gaurvi = 50 − (25 + 10) = 50 − 35 = 15

So, Archie's position from front is
= (10 + 8)th = 18th

16. (b)

Malini
17th
Reena Pallavi
31st 21st
27th

Malini's position 17th from left and 27th from right.

∴ Total number of girls = 17 + 27 − 1 = 43

17. (d) According to the question,

Q > R > T > P > S

Hence, 'S' read the newspaper last.

7. Direction Sense Test

1. (a) According to the question

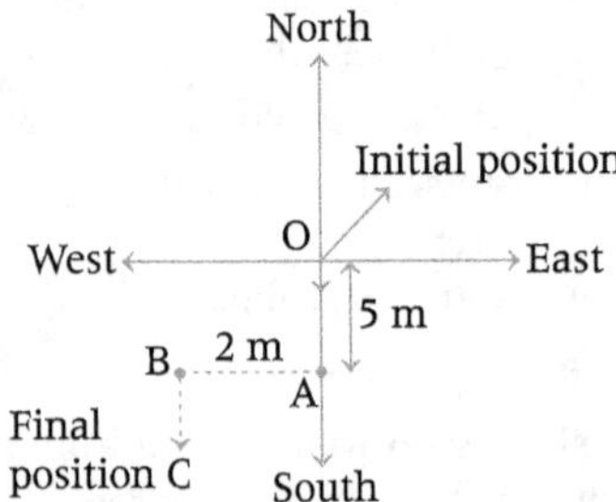

From the above figure, it is clear that Seema faces in the South direction.

Hence, option (a) is correct.

2. (c) Each direction moves 45° clockwise. So, East is called South-East.

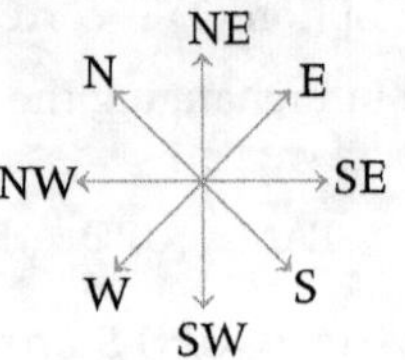

Hence, option (c) is correct.

3. (b) According to the question

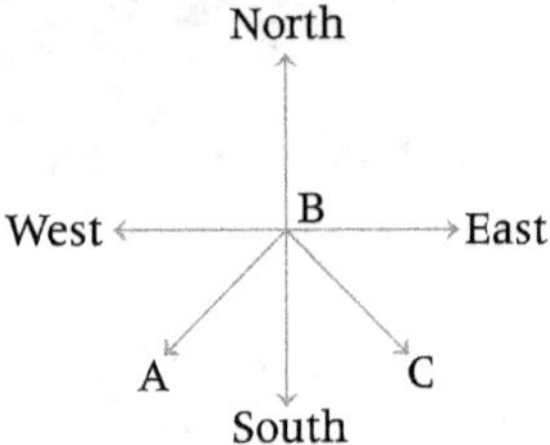

Clearly, C is to the East of A.
Hence, option (b) is correct.

4. (c) According to the question,

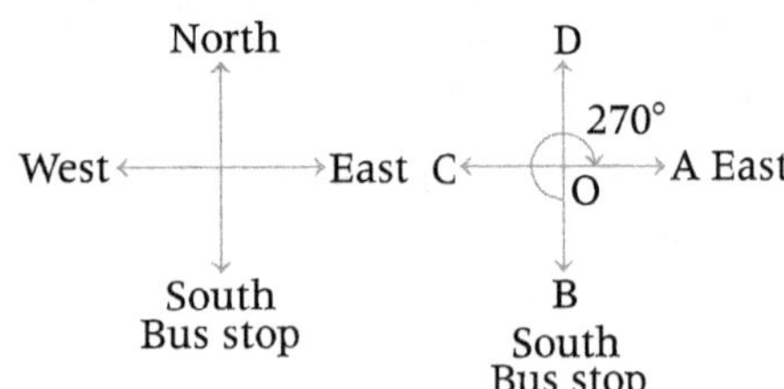

In the above figure, it is clear that, Kavita faces initially to OB i.e. South direction. To face East i.e. OA she initially moves to 90° clockwise i.e. OC, then next move to 90° clockwise i.e. OD and finally move to 90° clockwise i.e. OA.

So, to reach the East direction she moved
= 90° + 90° + 90° = 270°

Hence, option (c) is correct.

5. (c) According to the question,

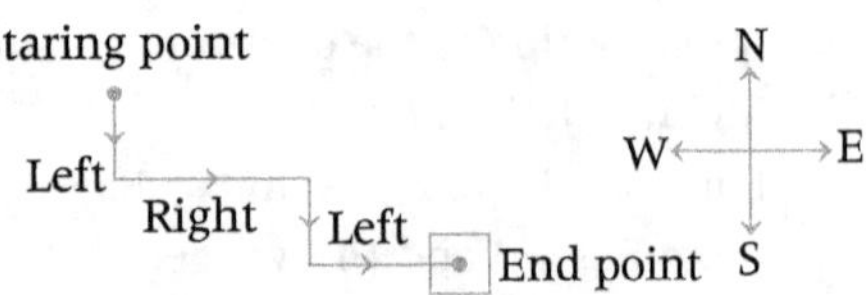

Clearly, he is moving in East direction.
Hence, option (c) is correct.

6. *(d)* According to the question,

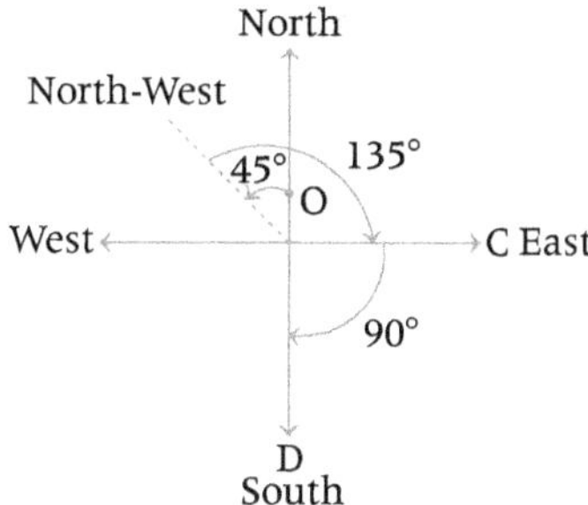

From the above figure, it is clear that Kamal initially faces in the North direction. On moving 45° anti-clockwise, he faces in North-West direction. On further moving 135° clockwise, he faces in the East. Finally, on moving 90° clockwise, he faces in the South direction .

Hence, option (d) is correct.

7. *(c)* According to the question,

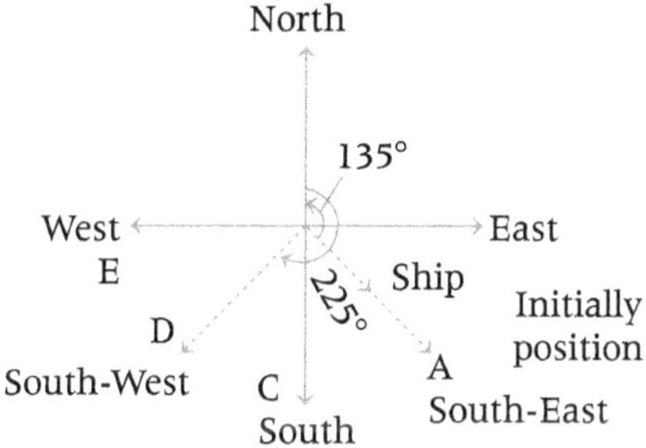

From the above figure, it is clear that ship is sailing in South-West.

Hence, option (c) is correct.

8. *(b)* According the question,

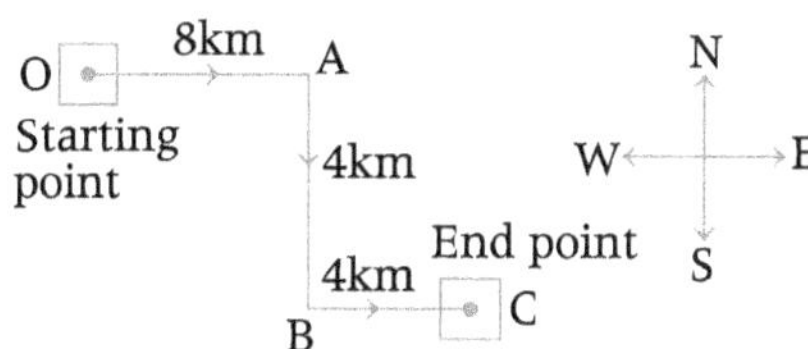

So, the total distance $= OA + AB + BC$

$= 8 + 4 + 4 = 16$ km

Hence, option (b) is correct.

9. *(d)* According to the question,

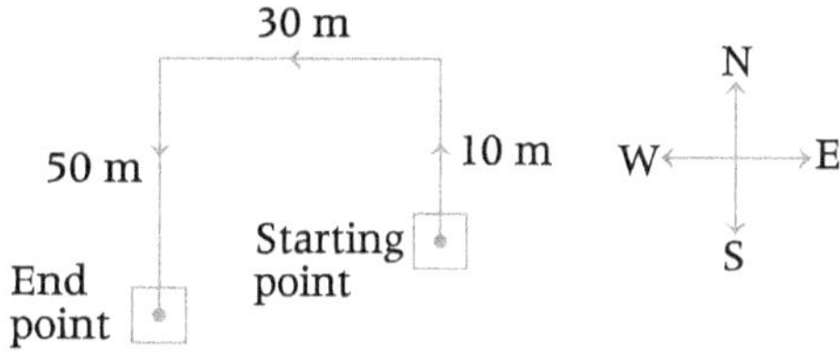

So, total distance $= 10 + 30 + 50 = 90$ m

Hence, option (d) is correct.

10. *(d)* According to the question,

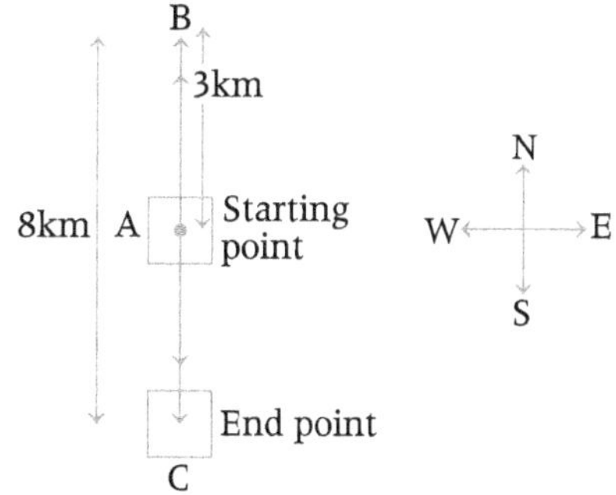

Here, we see that, the position of man at the end of the walk is towards South.

$\therefore$ Required distance $= BC - BA = 8 - 3 = 5$ km

Hence, option (d) is correct.

11. *(b)* According to the question,

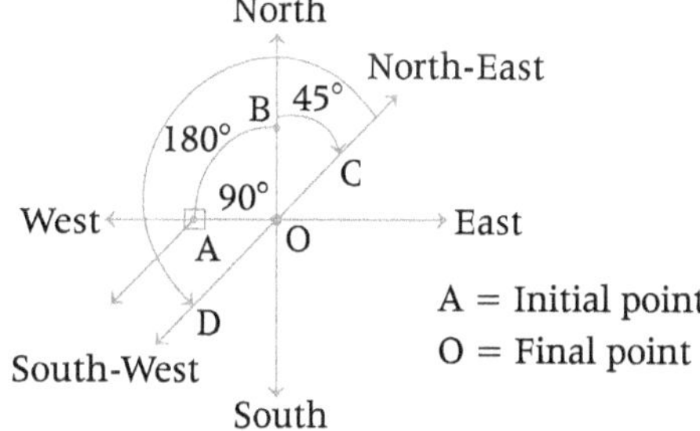

From the above figure, it is clear that Vikas initially faces in West direction. On moving 90° clockwise, he faces in the North direction. On further moving 45° clockwise, he faces in the North-East direction. Finally, on moving 180° anti-clockwise, he faces in the South-West direction.

Hence, option (b) is correct.

12. *(c)* According to the question,

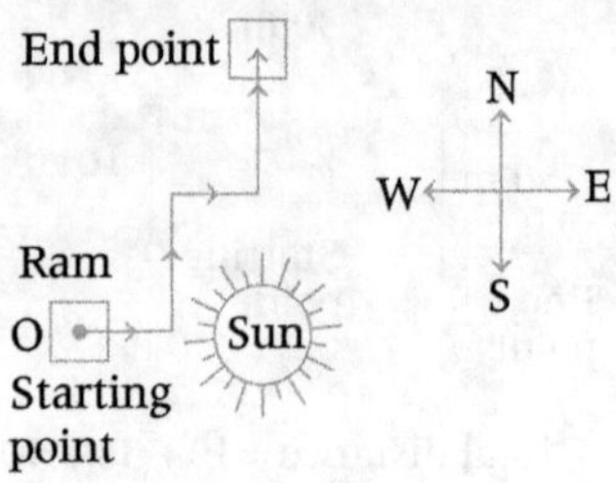

From the above figure it is clear that Ram is facing North direction.

Hence, option (c) is correct.

13. (c) According to the question,

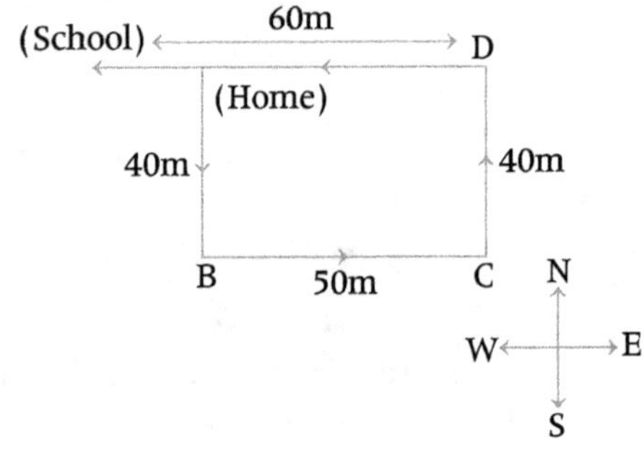

∴Distance between her school and home

$= (60 - 50)\text{ m} = 10\text{ m}$

Hence, option (c) is correct.

14. *(a)* According to the question,

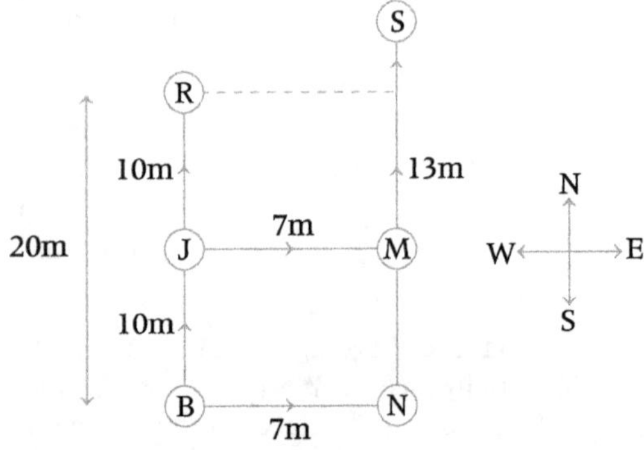

It's clear from the above diagram that the distance between S and N is

$= SM + MN$

$= (13 + 10)\text{ m} = 23\text{ m}$

and S is in North-East direction with respect to J. Hence option (a) is correct.

8. Blood Relations

1. *(c)* My father's father is my grandfather i.e. Mr. Rakesh. Meena is my sister. So, my grandfather is also Meena's grandfather. Therefore, Meena is the granddaughter of Mr. Rakesh. This can be represented as

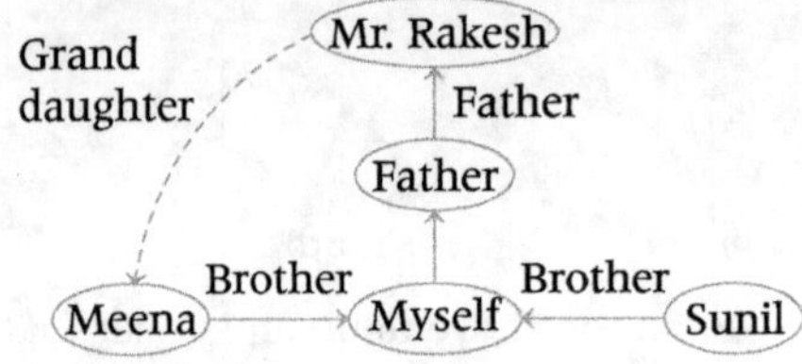

Hence, option (c) is correct.

2. *(d)* My father's real brother is my uncle i.e. Ramu. So, my real uncle is the son of my grandmother. This can be represented as

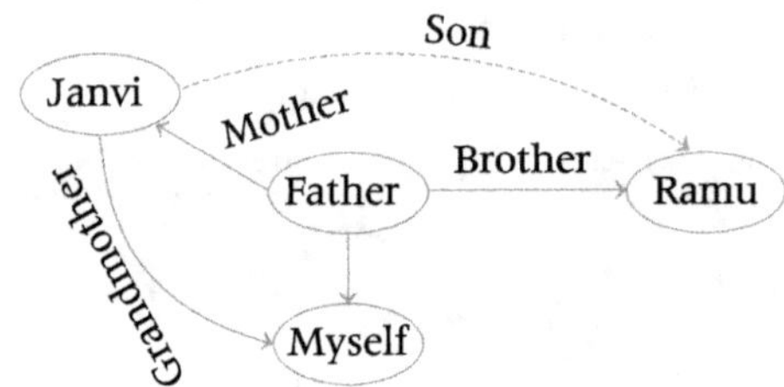

Hence, option (d) is correct.

3. *(b)* Seema is the daughter of Radhika and Mohan is her brother. Kirti is the wife of Mohan. So, Kirti is the aunt of Seema.

This can be represented as

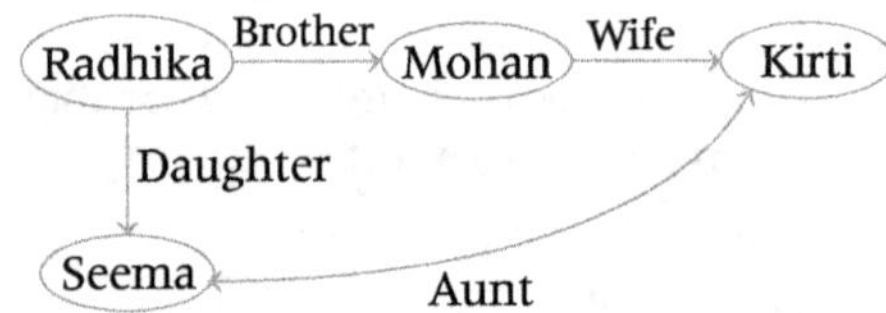

Hence, option (b) is correct.

4. *(d)* A is the sister of B, B is the brother of C and C is the father of D. Father's sister will be aunt. Therefore, A is the aunt of D.

This can be represented as

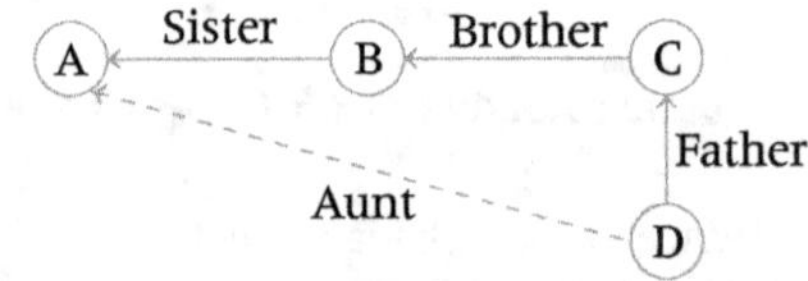

Hence, option (d) is correct.

5. *(b)* Radhika's sister's father is father of Radhika and the man in the photograph is the son of Radhika's father. So, Radhika is the sister of that man.

This can be represented as:

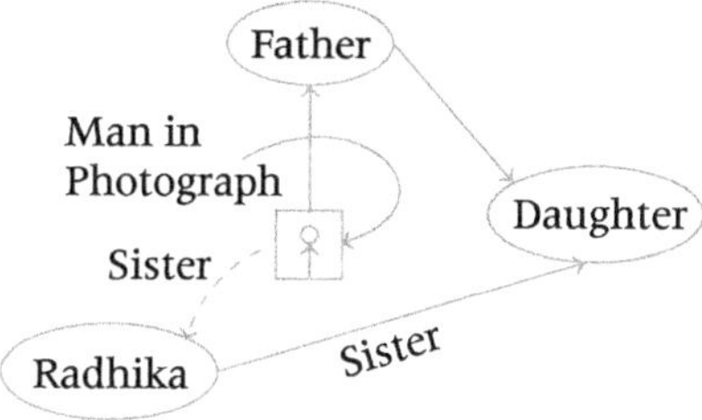

Hence, option (b) is correct.

6. *(d)* Only daughter of Kunal's mother-in-law means she is the wife of Kunal and daughter of Kunal's wife means Ayushi is the daughter of Kunal.

This can be represented as

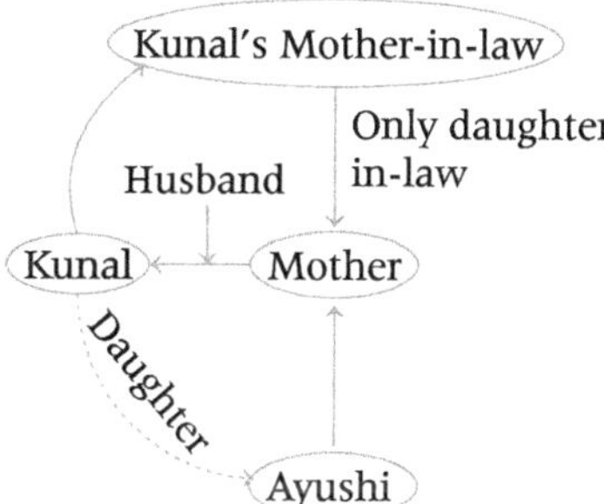

Hence, option (d) is correct.

7. *(d)* The only daughter of boy's mother's father is his mother herself. So, the boy is the son of that woman.

This can be represented as

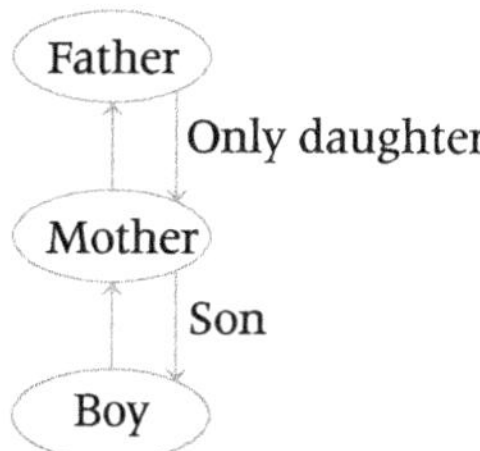

8. *(a)* Vimal's mother's husband is father of Vimal. Brother-in-law of Vimal's father is Vimal's uncle.

This can be represented as :

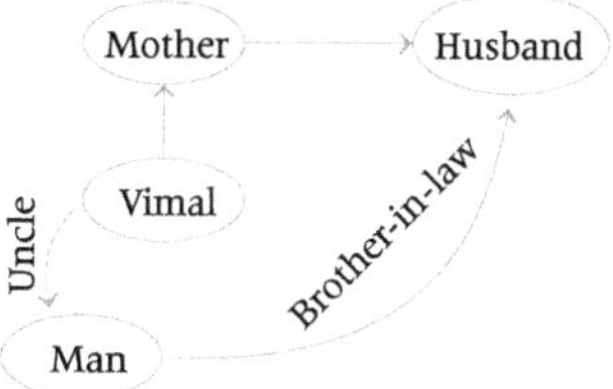

Hence, option (a) correct.

9. *(c)* Mother of Karan's son is the wife of Karan. Wife's sister is the sister-in-law. So, woman is the sister-in-law of Karan.

This can be represented as:

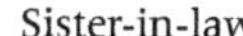

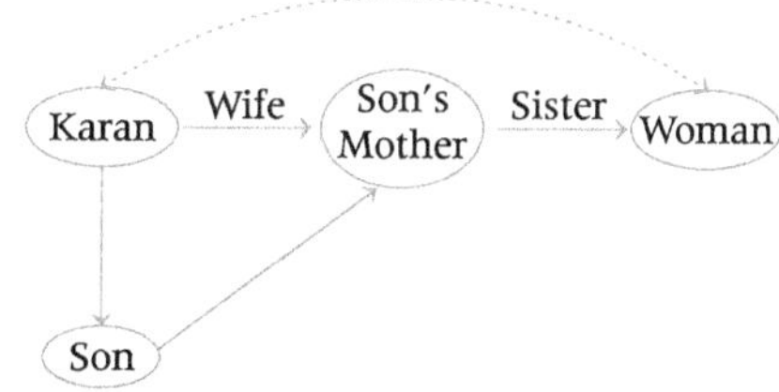

Hence, option (c) is correct.

10. *(a)* P's daughter is A's sister and A and B are brothers.

So, P is the mother of A and B. Q is the sister of B's mother, so she is his aunt.

The relation diagram can be drawn as

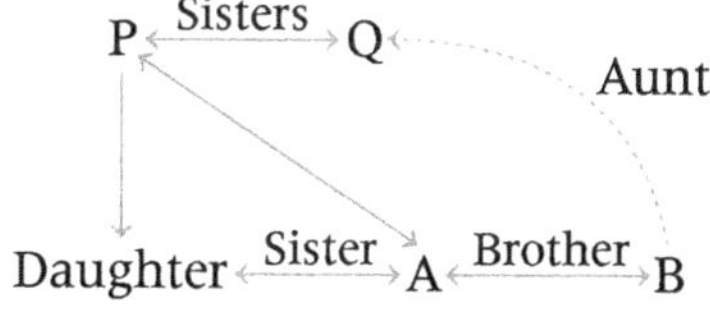

Hence, option (a) is correct.

11. *(b)* C's mother is also the mother of D and their mother is A's wife, so A is their father. B is A's brother, so he is their uncle. Therefore, D is B's nephew.

This can be represented as

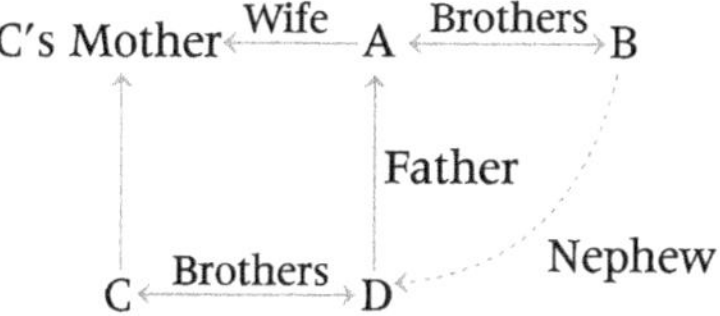

Hence, option (b) is correct.

12. *(d)* Esha is Bhavi's mother and Aditya is Bhavi's brother. Jayant is Aditya's brother, so Jayant is also Bhavi's brother.

So, Esha is mother of Jayant, Bhavi and Aditya.

Now, Bharat is father of Jayant, so he is husband of Esha. Therefore, Esha is Bharat's wife.

This can be represented as :

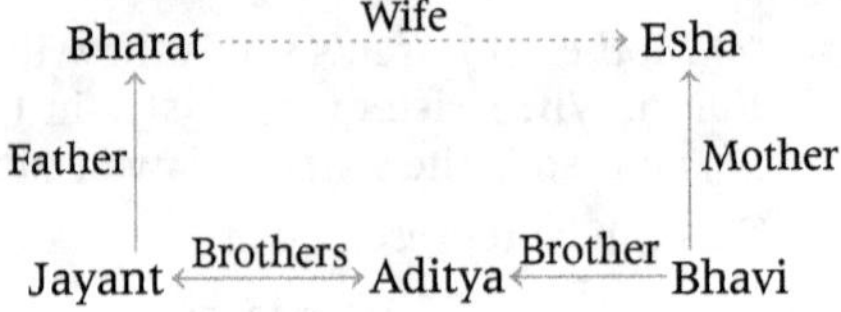

Hence, option (d) is correct.

13. *(b)* Varun is Sarika's brother, so he is Rahul's Maternal uncle and Ritesh is Rahul's maternal uncle's son, so he is his cousin.

This can be represented as

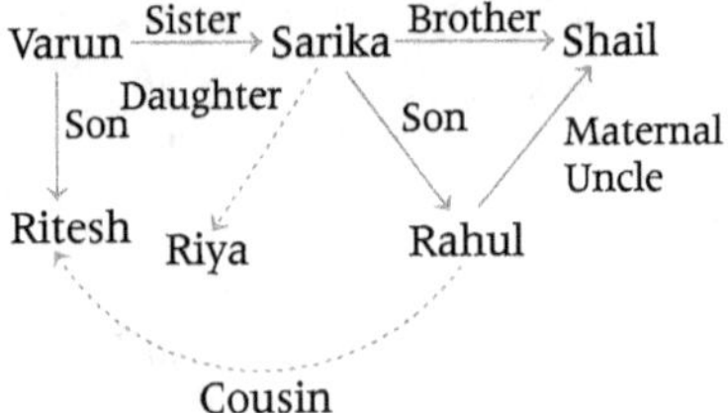

Hence, option (b) is correct.

Sol. (Q. Nos. 14 and 15) The diagram can be drawn as

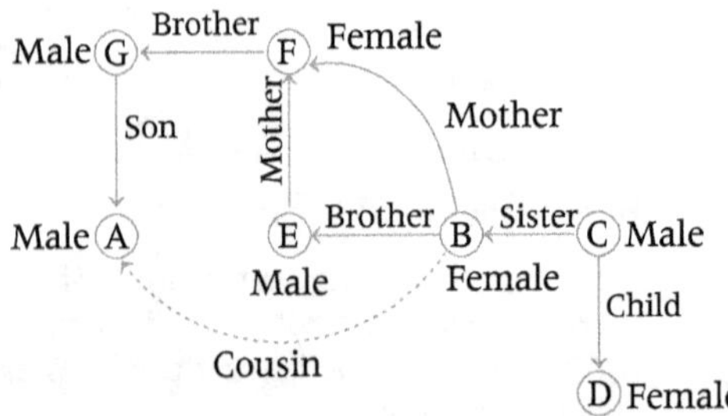

14. *(a)* According to the question, G is the brother of F and F is the mother of B, C and E.

So, G is the maternal uncle of B, C and E. A is the son of G. So, uncle's son i.e., A is the cousin of B, C and E.

Hence, option (a) is correct.

15. *(d)* When we observe the given options, we see except option (d) all options i.e., (a), (b) and (c) have one male and one female. In option (d), both F and B are females.

Hence, option (d) is correct.

16. *(d)* There are four male members in the family.

Hence, option (d) is correct.

17. *(c)* According to the question, G is the brother of F, C is the son of F. So, 'G' is the uncle of 'C'.

Hence, option (c) is correct.

9. Puzzles

Sol. (Q. Nos. 1 and 2) As per the given information, the data will arrange as shown below

	Intelligent	Hard-working	Honest	Ambitious
Kailash	✓	✓	✗	✓
Govind	✓	✗	✗	✓
Harinder	✓	✗	✓	✗
Rajesh	✗	✓	✓	✗
Jitendra	✗	✓	✓	✓

1. *(c)* From the above table, we find that Harinder is neither hard-working nor ambitious. Hence, option (c) is correct.

2. *(b)* From the above table, we find that Govind is neither honest nor hard-working, but is ambitious. Hence, option (b) is correct.

Sol. (Q. Nos. 3-5) As per the given information, the data will arranged as shown below.

3. (b) From the above arrangement, it is clear that Rani is in the middle position on the bench. Hence, option (b) is correct.

4. (d) From the above arrangement, it is clear that Seema is second from the left end of the bench. Hence, option (d) is correct.

5. (c) From the above arrangement, it is clear that Reeta is second from right end. Hence, option (c) is correct.

Sol. (Q. Nos. 6 and 7) As per the given information, circle will arranged as shown below.

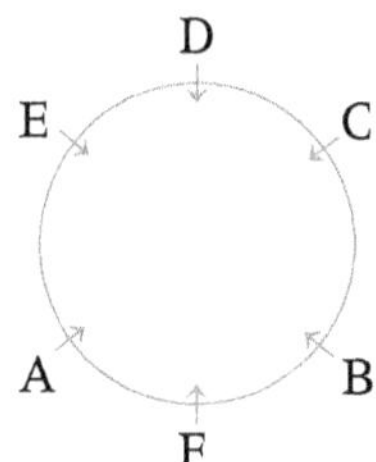

6. (b) From the above figure, it is clear that the neighbours of B are C and F.
Hence, option (b) is correct.

7. (c) From the above figure, it is clear that F is second to the right of E. Hence, option (c) is correct.

Sol. (Q. Nos 8-10) As per the given information the data will be arranged as shown below.

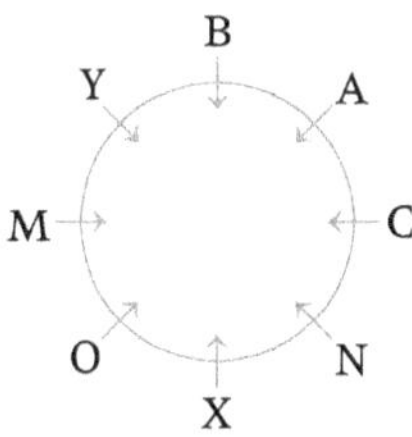

8. *(a)* According to the figure, 'M' is between 'O' and 'Y'. Hence, option (a) is correct.

9. (a) According to the figure, 'C' is not neighbour of 'X'.
Hence, option (a) is correct.

10. *(c)* According to the question, 'B' is to the immediate left of 'Y'.
Hence, option (c) is correct.

Sol. (Q. Nos. 11-13)As per the given information the data will be arranged as shown below.

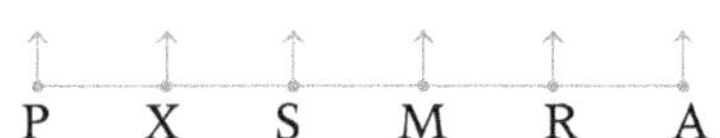

11. (b) According to the figure, X is immediate right of P. Hence, option (b) is correct.

12. (a) A sits first from the right end.
Hence, option (a) is correct.

13. (c) According to the figure, 'XS' are immediate neighbour to each other.
Hence, option (c) is correct.

Sol. (Q. Nos. 14-16) As per the given information, the data will arrange as shown below.

Teachers → **↓ Subjects**	**A**	**B**	**C**	**D**	**E**
Hindi	✓	✓	✗	✓	✗
English	✓	✓	✓	✗	✗
Mathematics	✓	✗	✗	✓	✗
History	✗	✓	✗	✗	✓
French	✗	✓	✗	✗	✓
Geography	✗	✓	✓	✗	✗

14. (b) From the above table, it is clear that B is teaching maximum number of subjects.
Hence, option (b) is correct.

15. (d) From the above table, it is clear that Hindi and English are taught by more than two teachers. Hence, option (d) is correct.

16. (c) From the above table, it is clear that teachers D, B and A teach the Hindi subject only. Hence, option (c) is correct.

17. (d) As per the given information, the data will arranged as shown below.

$$2 \xrightarrow{+1} 3 \xrightarrow{+1} 4$$

Maya   Suraj/Tiya   Samsul   Tiya/Suraj   Ankit   ↑ East

Now, when Tiya is fourth from the left end

Maya   Suraj   Samsul   Tiya   Ankit

Then, Suraj is fourth from the right end.
Hence, option (d) is correct.

10. Mathematical Reasoning

1. *(b)* We have, $24 + 2 \times 4 \div 6 - 3$
On substituting the signs, we get
$$24 \times 2 - 4 + 6 \div 3$$
Simplify the above expression using VBODMAS rule,
$24 \times 2 - 4 + 6 \div 3$
$= 24 \times 2 - 4 + 2 = 48 - 4 + 2 = 50 - 4 = 46$
Hence, option (b) is correct.

2. *(c)* We have, $5 \times 4 \div 6 + 5 - 4$
On substituting the signs, we get

$5-4+6\times5\div4$

Simplify the above expression using VBODMAS rule,

$5-4+6\times5\div4$

$=5-4+6\times\frac{5}{4}=5-4+6\times1.25$

$=5-4+7.5=12.5-4=8.5$

Hence, option (c) is correct.

3. *(b)* We have, $350-50\div10+40\times6+20$

On substituting the sign, we get

$350\div50+10\times40-6\times20$

Simplify the above expression using VBODMAS rule,

$350\div50+10\times40-6\times20$

$=7+10\times40-6\times20$

$=7+400-120=407-120=287$

Hence, option (b) is correct.

4. *(b)* Here, the rule applied is

$x * y = x^y$

As, $2*3=2^3=8$, $3*2=3^2=9$

and $5*1=5^1=5$

Similarly, $4*3=4^3=64$

Hence, option (b) is correct.

5. (b) As, $6\bigstar5=6\times5+1=31$

$7\bigstar8=7\times8+1=57$

and $3\bigstar4=3\times4+1=13$

Similarly, $9\bigstar10=9\times10+1=91$

Hence, option (b) is correct.

6. *(c)* Given, $P\times Q+R\div S$

Now, on putting the value of the letters, we get $8\times5+14\div7=8\times5+2=40+2=42$

Hence, option (c) is correct.

7. *(d)* We have given, $(9\ \&\ 3)\#12@10$

Now, on putting the values of symbols, we get $(9\ \&\ 3)\#12@10=(9\times3)-12+10$

$=27-12+10=37-12=25$

Hence, option (d) is correct.

8. *(a)* We have given,

$25@2@6=4@11@0$

by option (a) we get,

$25\times2-6=4\times11+0$

$50-6=44+0\Rightarrow 44=44$

Clearly, LHS = RHS

Hence, option (a) is correct.

9. *(a)* From option (a), applying the interchanges, the equation will be

$4\times2+5=8+5=13$

Hence, option (a) is correct.

10. *(c)* By option (c), we get

$15\div3\times8=40$

$5\times8=40$

$40=40$

LHS = RHS

11. *(a)* After interchanging the signs as given in option (a),

$\text{LHS}=50\div5\times4+4$

$=10\times4+4$

$=40+4=44$ RHS

LHS = RHS

Hence, option (a) is correct.

12. *(b)* According to the question,

Mohan can walk in 11 h = 121 km

Mohan can walk in 1 h $=\frac{121}{11}$ km $=11$ km

$\therefore$ Mohan can walk in 6 h $=(11\times6)$ km

$=66$ km

Hence, option (b) is correct.

13. *(c)* According to the question,

Rice consumed by 240 students in a month

$=1440$ kg

Rice consumed by 1 student in a month

$=\frac{1440}{240}=6$ kg

$\therefore$ Rice consumed by 150 students in a month will be $=(6\times150)$ kg $=900$ kg

Hence, option (c) is correct.

14. *(b)* According to the question,

$\because$ The cost of 90 L of petrol = ₹ 5400

$\therefore$ The cost of 1 L of petrol $=\frac{5400}{90}=$ ₹ 60

$\therefore$ The cost of 18 L of petrol will be $=(18\times60)$

$=$ ₹ 1080

Hence, option (b) is correct.

15. *(c)* We have,

$(32\div128-16\times8+4)-(4+30\div30-6\times16)$

On substituting the sign, we get

$(32 + 128 \div 16 - 8 \times 4) \div (4 \times 30 + 30 \div 6 - 16)$

Simplify the above expression using VBODMAS rule,

$= (32 + 128 \div 16 - 8 \times 4) \div (4 \times 30 + 30 \div 6 - 16)$

$= (32 + 8 - 8 \times 4) \div (4 \times 30 + 5 - 16)$

$= (32 + 8 - 32) \div (120 + 5 - 16)$

$= (40 - 32) \div (125 - 16)$

$= 8 \div 109 = 8/109$

Hence, option (c) is correct.

16. *(b)* We have given, 35#15%40$10@5

Now on putting the values of symbol we get, $35 - 15 + 40 \div 10 \times 5$

$= 35 - 15 + 4 \times 5 = 35 - 15 + 20$

$= 55 - 15 = 40$

Hence, option (b) is correct.

17. *(c)* We have, $1 \uparrow 41 \leftarrow 5 \uparrow 37 \downarrow 91 \rightarrow 7$

On substituting the values of the given signs, we get $1 + 41 \times 5 + 37 - 91 \div 7$

Simplify the above expression using VBODMAS rule,

$1 + 41 \times 5 + 37 - 91 \div 7 = 1 + 41 \times 5 + 37 - 13$

$= 1 + 205 + 37 - 13 = 243 - 13 = 230$

Hence, option (c) is correct.

18. *(c)* According to the question,

The annual rent of Mr. Gupta's house is ₹3600.

We know that, there are 12 months in a year.

$\therefore$ The rent for one month $= \frac{3600}{12} =$ ₹ 300

So, the rent for 5 months will be

= ₹(300 × 5) = ₹1500

Hence, option (c) is correct.

11. Inserting the Missing Characters

1. *(a)* In each row, middle number = (sum of the two outer numbers)/2

In I row, $(6 + 8)/2 = 7$

In II row, $(10 + 22)/2 = 16$

Similarly, in III row, $(8 + 6)/2 = \boxed{7}$

Hence, option (a) is correct.

2. *(b)* In figure I, $(10 + 15 + 5)/10 = 30/10 = 3$

In figure II, $(18 + 11 + 11)/10 = 40/10 = 4$

Similarly, in figure III,

$(19 + 20 + 21)/10 = 60/10 = \boxed{6}$

Hence, option (b) is correct.

3. *(b)* Here, the number written on the left side of the line is the square of the number written on right side.

As, $1^2 = 1$ and $5^2 = 25$

Similarly, $9^2 = \boxed{81}$

Hence, option (b) is correct.

4. *(d)* In figure I, $16 + 20 = 36$

and $36 + 4 = 40$

In figure II, $25 + 21 = 46$

and $46 + 4 = 50$

Similarly, in figure III,

$32 + 23 = 55$ and $55 + 4 = \boxed{59}$

Hence, option (d) is correct.

5. *(c)* In figure I, $(2 \times 9) - (3 \times 6) = 18 - 18 = 0$

In figure II, $(2 \times 11) - (5 \times 4) = 22 - 20 = 2$

Similarly, in figure III,

$(7 \times 7) - (8 \times 6) = 49 - 48 = \boxed{1}$

Hence, option (c) is correct.

6. *(d)* Here, the addition of the numbers written in circles gives the positional value of the letter written in square as shown below :

$1 + 3 = 4 \rightarrow$ (D), $5 + 4 = 9 \rightarrow$ (I)

Similarly, $11 + 10 = 21 \rightarrow$ (U)

Hence, option (d) is correct.

7. *(b)* In each figure, the numbers inside the box are multiplied to give the number outside.

Box 1 : $2 \times 6 \times 5 \times 1 = 60$

Box 2 : $3 \times 5 \times 2 \times 4 = 120$

Similarly, Box 3 : $5 \times 5 \times 4 \times 4 = \boxed{400}$

Hence, option (b) is correct.

8. *(b)* In figure I,

$(9 \times 3) + 3 = 30$

In figure III,

$(7 \times 8) + 4 = 60$

Similarly, in figure II, $(8 \times 2) + 4 = X$

$\Rightarrow X = 20$

$\therefore X^2 - 1 = 20^2 - 1 = 400 - 1 = 399$

Hence, option (b) is correct.

9. *(b)* In left semi-circle, moving anti-clockwise starting from 7 and in right semi-circle, moving clockwise starting from G, each number represents the postitional value in english alphabetical order of the corresponding letter.
So, the positional value of Q i.e. 17 will be the missing number.
Hence, option (b) is correct.

10. *(b)* As, $(2\times2)-1=3, (3\times2)-1=5, (5\times2)-1=9$
Similarly, $(9\times2)-1=\boxed{17}$
Hence, option (b) is correct.

11. *(b)* If figure I,
$11^2+7^2+9^2+4^2=121+49+81+16=267$
In figure II,
$5^2+12^2+8^2+3^2=25+144+64+9=242$
Similarly,
In figure III
$7^2+4^2+6^2+14^2=49+16+36+196=\boxed{297}$
Hence, option (b) is correct.

12. *(c)* Here, the (multiplication –2) of the numbers written in the middle circle,
From I, $(5\times4\times3\times2)-2=118$
From II, $(1\times8\times2\times6)-2=94$
Similarly, $(5\times4\times2\times3)-2=\boxed{118}$
Hence, option (c) is correct.

13. *(d)* In circle I,
$$(12-4)\times4=8\times4=32$$
In circle II,
$$(18-9)\times4=9\times4=36$$
Similarly, in circle III,
$$(23-4)\times4=19\times4=\boxed{76}$$
Hence, option (d) is correct.

14. *(a)* When we move in clockwise direction from 11 to 6, we get a pattern,
As, $(11+5)^2=(16)^2=256$
$(8+4)^2=(12)^2=144$
$(3+7)^2=(10)^2=100$
Similarly, $(12+6)^2=(18)^2=\boxed{324}$
Hence, option (a) is correct.

15. *(a)* In figure I, $(2\times4)+(5\times3)=8+15=23$
In figure II, $(1\times6)+(8\times4)=6+32=38$
Similarly, in figure III,
$$(3\times7)+(11\times2)=21+22=\boxed{43}$$
Hence, option (a) is correct.

16. *(a)* Here, the letters follow the pattern given below
Considering rowwise,
In I row, $A\xrightarrow{+6}G\xrightarrow{+6}M$
In II row, $C\xrightarrow{+6}I\xrightarrow{+6}\boxed{O}$
In III row, $E\xrightarrow{+6}K\xrightarrow{+6}Q$
Hence, option (a) is correct.

17. (c) Here,
In I row, $Z\xrightarrow{-2}X\xrightarrow{-2}V$
In II row, $A\xrightarrow{-2}Y\xrightarrow{-2}\boxed{W}$
In III row, $T\xrightarrow{-2}R\xrightarrow{-2}P$
So, I column,
$$2\xrightarrow{+1}3\xrightarrow{+1}4$$
In II column,
$$19\xrightarrow{+1}20\xrightarrow{+1}21$$
In III column,
$$66\xrightarrow{+1}\boxed{67}\xrightarrow{+1}68$$
So, the missing number is W_{67}.
Hence, option (c) is correct

18. *(c)* In triangle I,
$12-5=7$
$19-12=7$
$19-5=14$
In triangle II,
$13-7=6$
$23-13=10$
$23-7=16$
Similarly, in triangle III,
$11-4=7$
$18-11=\boxed{7}$
$18-4=14$
Hence, option (c) is correct.

14. Paper Folding and Paper Cutting

1. *(c)* The folded transparent sheet will appear as

Hence, option (c) is correct.

2. *(b)* The folded transparent sheet will appear as

Hence, option (b) is correct.

3. *(c)* The folded transparent sheet will appear as

Hence, option (c) is correct.

4. *(a)* The folded transparent sheet will appear as

Hence, option (a) is correct.

5. *(c)* The folded transparent sheet will appear as

Hence, option (c) is correct.

6. *(c)* Upon unfolding the folded paper, represented by figure (Z) will look like as

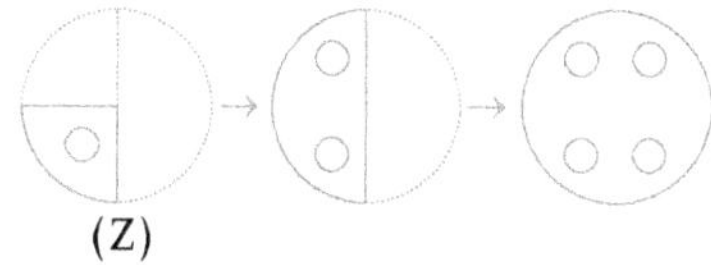

Hence, option (c) is correct.

7. *(a)* Upon unfolding the folded paper, represented by figure (Z) will look like as

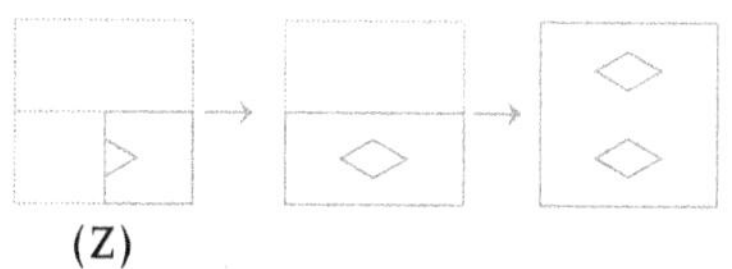

Hence, option (a) is correct.

8. (a) Upon unfolding the folded paper, represented by figure (Z) will look like as:

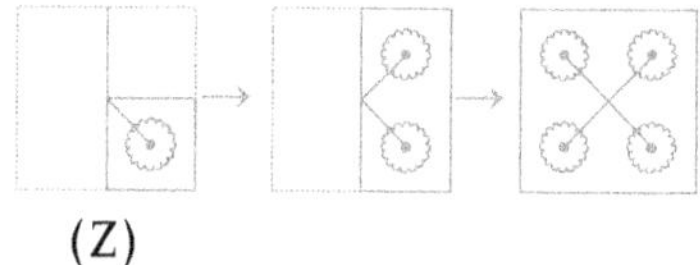

Hence, option (a) is correct.

9. (a) The folded transparent sheet will appear as

Hence, option (a) is correct.

10. *(d)* The folded transparent sheet will appear as

Hence, option (d) is correct.

11. (c) Upon unfolding the folded paper, represented by figure (Z) will look like as:

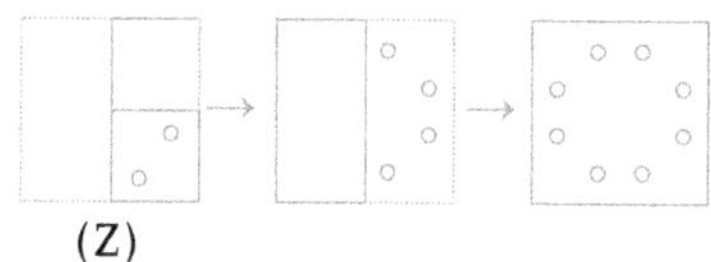

Hence, option (c) is correct.

12. (b) Option figure (b) most would be closely resemble the unfolded form of figure (Z).

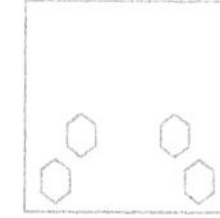

Hence, option (b) is correct.

15. Embedded Figures and Figure Formation

1. *(b)* The given figure (X) can be traced out in figure (b) as shown below:

Hence, option (b) is correct.

2. *(c)* The given figure (X) can be traced out in figure (c) as shown below

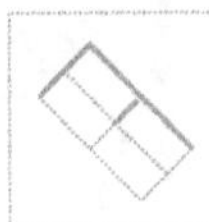

Hence, option (c) is correct.

3. *(a)* The given figure (X) can be traced out in figure (a) as shown below:

Hence, option (a) is correct.

4. *(b)* From the given options, figure (b) will be formed by joining all the pieces of figure (X), as shown below:

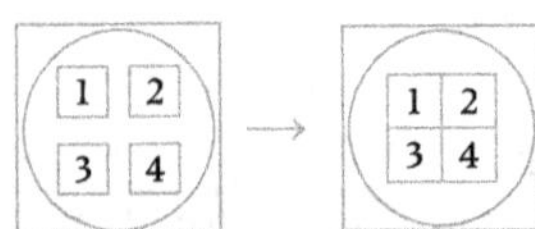

Hence, option (b) is correct.

5. *(c)* From the given options, figure (c) will be formed by joining all the pieces of figure (X), as shown below:

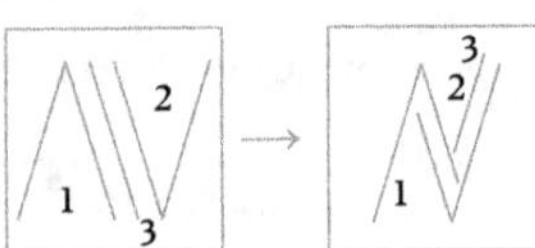

Hence, option (c) is correct.

6. *(d)* After close observation, we see that, figure (d) has the same components as that of the figure (X).

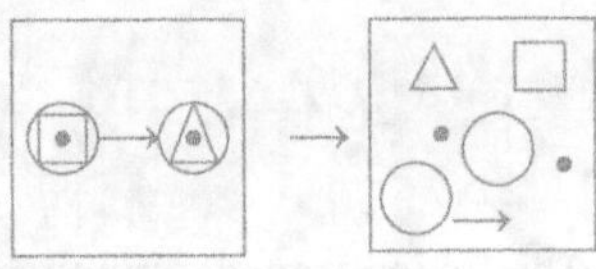

Hence, option (d) is correct.

7. *(a)* After close observation, we see that figure (a) has the same components as that of the figure (X).

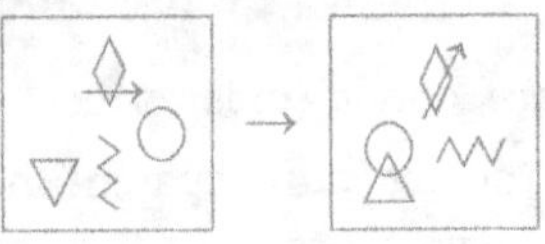

Hence, option (a) is correct.

8. *(a)* After close observation, we find that figure (a) exactly fits into figure (X) to form a perfect square.

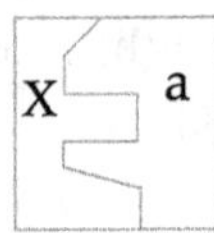

Hence, option (a) is correct.

9. *(b)* After close observation, we find that figure (b) exactly fits into figure (X) to form a perfect square.

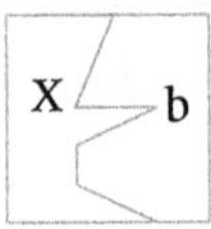

Hence, option (b) is correct.

10. *(b)* After close observation, we find that figure (b) exactly fits into figure (X) to form a perfect square.

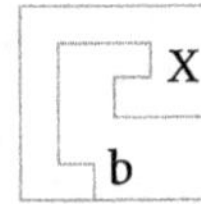

Hence, option (b) is correct.

11. *(b)* In figures (1), (6) and (8) shapes are divided into two parts and having two black dots. In figures (2), (3) and (9) the shapes are shaded by vertical lines. In figures (4), (5) and (7) same shapes are intersecting each other. Thus, three groups are (1, 6, 8); (2, 3, 9) and (4, 5, 7) Hence, option (b) is correct.

12. *(c)* Figures (1), (8) and (6) are composed in circle with different shapes.

Figures (2), (7) and (9) are divided into two equal parts and (3), (4) and (5) are shaded with short lines. So, three groups are (1, 8, 6); (2, 7, 9) and (3, 5, 4).

Hence, option (c) is correct.

13. *(a)* (1, 4), (2, 3) and (5, 6) are three different pairs of identical figures.

Hence, option (a) is correct.

14. *(c)* The given figure (X) can be traced out in figure (c) as shown below:

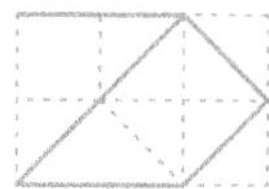

Hence, option (c) is correct.

15. *(c)* From the given options, figure (c) will be formed by joining all the pieces of figure (X) as shown below :

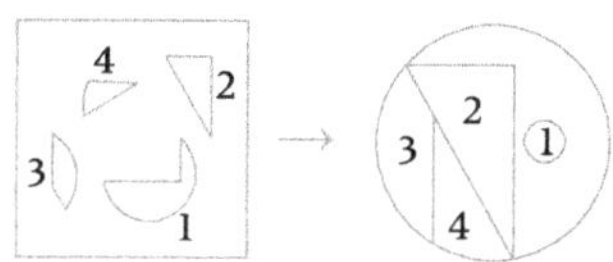

Hence, option (c) is correct.

16. *(a)* After close observation, we see that, figure (a) has the same components as that of the figure (X).

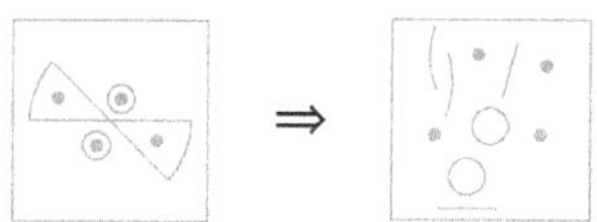

Hence, option (a) is correct.

17. *(d)* After close observation, we find that figure (d) exactly fits into figure (X) to form a perfect square.

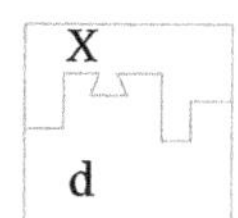

Hence, option (d) is correct.

18. *(c)* After close observation, we find that figure (c) exactly fits into figure (X) to form a perfect square.

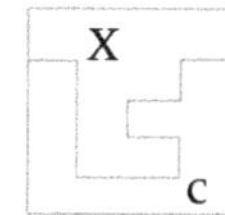

Hence, option (c) is correct.

19. *(a)* (1), (3) and (9) have one element placed inside a different element.

Figures (2), (5) and (6) contain two mutually perpendicular lines dividing the figure into four parts.

Figures (4), (7) and (8) have two similar elements (unequal in size) attached to each other. So, three groups are (1, 3, 9) : (12, 5, 6) and (4, 7, 8).

Hence, option (a) is correct.

Practice Set-1

1. *(b)* The series can be represented as

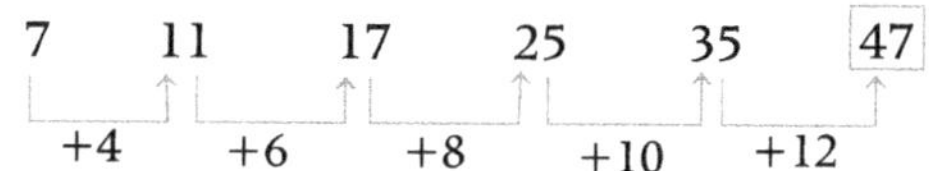

Hence, option (b) is correct.

2. *(c)* As,

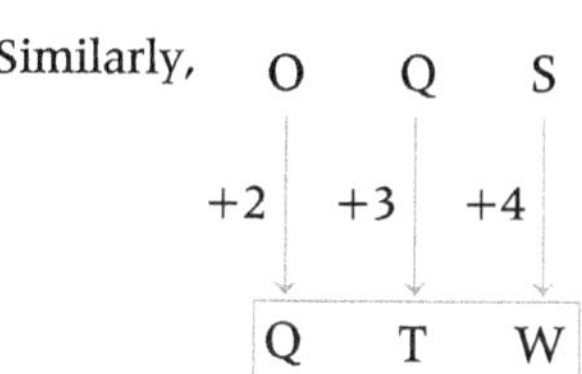

3. *(a)* In figure I, $8 + 4 = 12$

and $\frac{12}{4} = 3$

In figure II, $10 + 10 = 20$

and $\frac{20}{4} = 5$

Similarly in figure III, $15 + 9 = 24$

and $\frac{24}{4} = 6$

Hence, option (a) is correct.

4. *(b)* The correct mirror image is

NAME25 | ƧƧƎMAИ

Hence, option (b) is correct.

5. *(a)* We have, $125 \times 25 + 20 - 80$

On substituting the symbols as given in question, we get

$125 \div 25 \times 20 + 80 = 5 \times 20 + 80$ $(\because 125 \div 25 = 5)$

$= 100 + 80$ $(\because 5 \times 20 = 100)$

$= 180$

Hence, option (a) is correct.

6. *(c)* This can be represented as

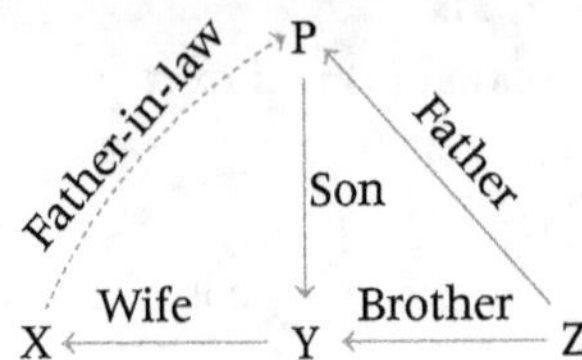

Hence, option (c) is correct.

7. *(c)* In first pair, the part of the circle is removed from first figure to second figure. On following this pattern (c) will complete the second pair.

Hence, option (c) is correct.

8. *(b)* In all the figures, except figure (b) the number of lines in outer shape is one less than the number of lines in inner shape. But in figure (b) the number of lines in outer shape is two less than the number of lines in inner shape.
So, figure (b) is odd one.
Hence, option (b) is correct.

9. *(d)* The information given in question can be represented as

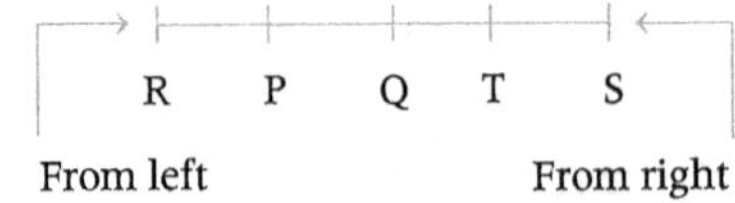

Clearly, P is fourth from the right.

Hence, option (d) is correct.

10. *(b)* Except, Hale all other are end with ail.
So, Hale is odd one.
Hence, option (b) is correct.

11. *(b)* The transparent sheet will appear as

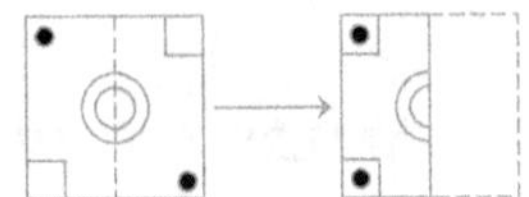

Hence, option (b) is correct.

12. *(d)* The given figure (X) is embedded in figure (d) as shown below

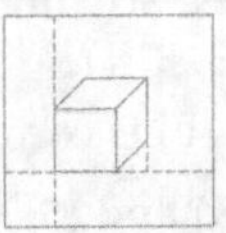

Hence, option (d) is correct.

13. *(c)* According to the question,

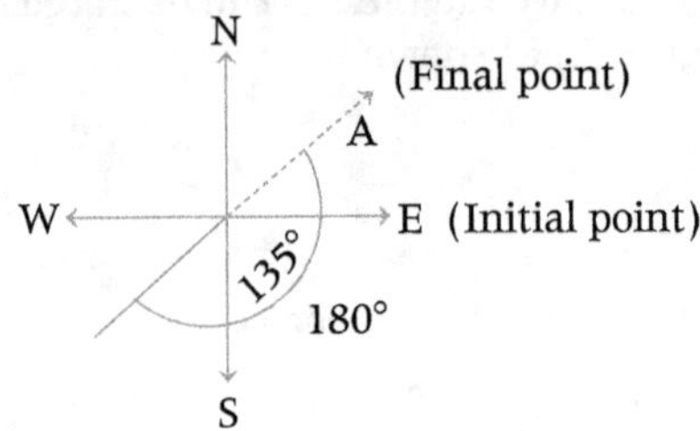

Clearly, he turned 135° clockwise direction and then 180° in anti-clockwise.
So, now he is facing North-East.
Hence, option (c) is correct.

14. *(a)* As,

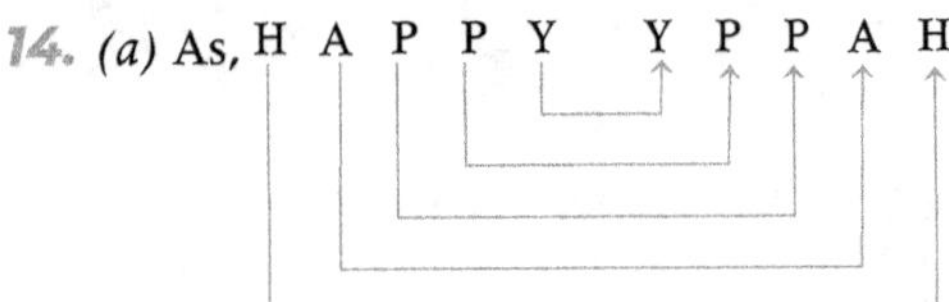

Similarly,

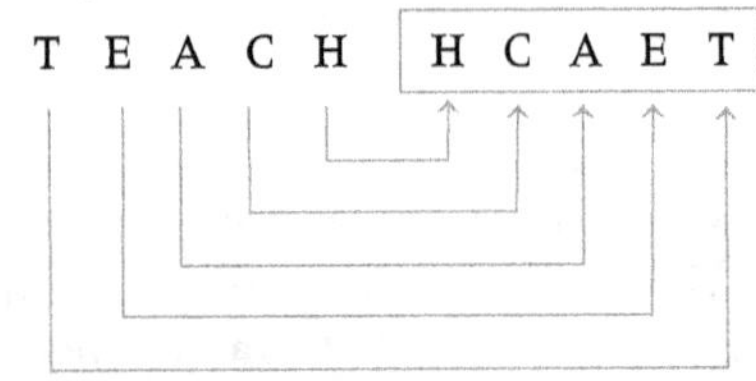

Hence, option (a) is correct.

15. *(c)* As 'chapter' is a part of the 'book', similarly 'brick' is a part of a 'building'.

Hence, option (c) is correct.

16. *(a)* The pattern can be represented as

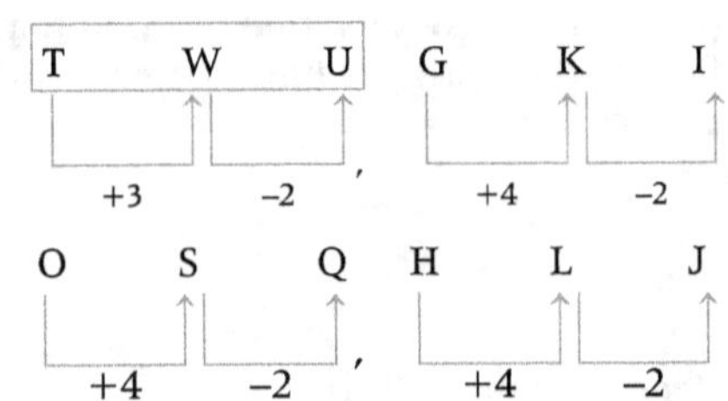

All the groups, except TWU follow similar pattern, but TWU follow different pattern.

So, group TWU is odd one.

Hence, option (a) is correct.

17. *(d)* The pattern is as follows

$$L \xrightarrow{+2} N \xrightarrow{+3} Q \xrightarrow{+4} U \xrightarrow{+5} \boxed{Z}$$

So, Z will come next.

Hence, option (d) is correct.

18. *(b)* The letters are coded as

Letters	S	L	O	W	T	A	K	E
Numbers	I	5	9	8	2	4	3	7

Here, $L \rightarrow 5, A \rightarrow 4, T \rightarrow 2$ and $E \rightarrow 7$

So, the code for LATE is 5427.

Hence, option (b) is correct.

19. *(a)* As, $25+15=40, 32+8=40,$

$28+12=40$ and $?+2=40$

$\therefore \quad ?=40-2=38$

So, 38 is the missing number.

Hence, option (a) is correct.

20. *(d)* On rearranging the letters given in option, we get

Option (a) QUICK, option (b) BREAK, Option (c) DAMAGE and option (d) CURE. Among these, only CURE is a synonym of 'Heal'.

Hence, option (d) is correct.

21. *(a)* As, $7*8=7\times8=56$

$6*9=6\times9=54$

and $4*6=64\times6=24$

Similarly, $11*5=11\times5=\boxed{55}$

Hence, option (a) is correct.

22. *(b)* The direction graph can be drawn as

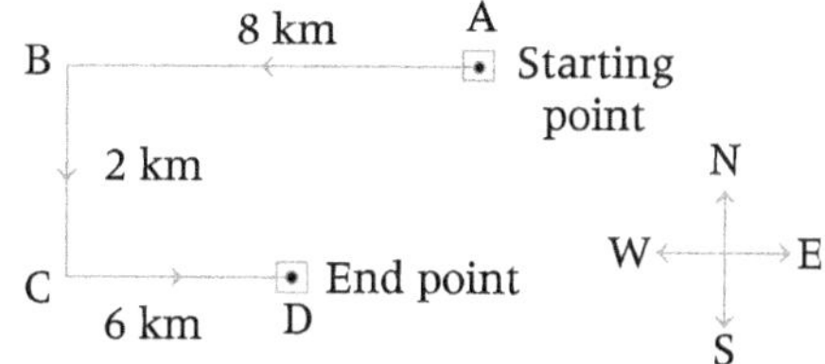

Now, total distance covered by Akanksha $= AB+BC+CD=8+2+6=16$ km

Hence, option (b) is correct.

23. *(c)* This can be represented as

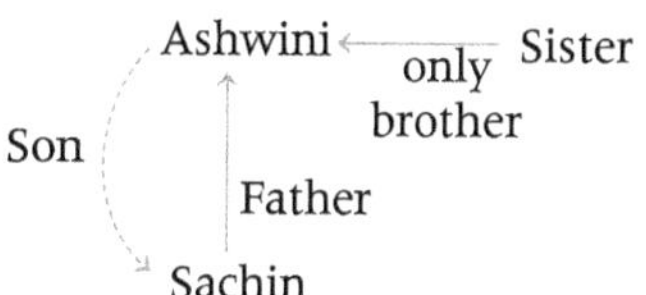

Hence, option (c) is correct.

24. *(b)*

25. *(a)* The outer arc is rotating 90° in clockwise direction and the inner arc is rotating 90° in anti-clockwise direction in each step. On following this pattern, option figure (a) will complete the series.

Hence, option (a) is correct.

26. *(a)* The lines used to make the first figure is reduced by one and the new formed figure is enclosed within a circle. On following this pattern, option figure (a) will complete the second pair.

Hence, option (a) is correct.

27. *(b)*

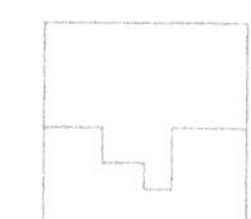

Hence, option (b) is correct.

28. *(c)* On folding the given transparent sheet, we get

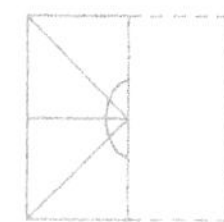

Hence, option (c) is correct.

29. *(c)* The correct mirror image of the given figure is

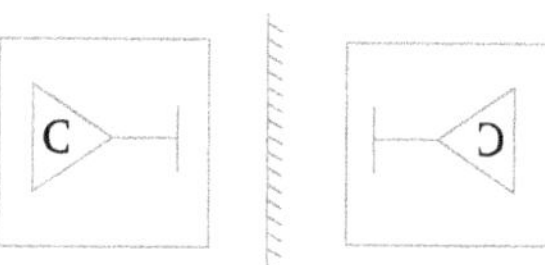

Hence, option (c) is correct.

30. *(c)* On putting the values, we get $4+8+2=14$, which is equal to P.
Hence, option (c) is correct.

31. *(b)* We can see that, letters' group BC, GH and WX have consecutive letters while letters' group KM does not have consecutive letters. So KM is different from others.
Hence, option (b) is correct.

32. *(a)* The given series can be represented as

$A \xrightarrow{+1} B \xrightarrow{+2} D \xrightarrow{+3} G \xrightarrow{+4} K \xrightarrow{+5} \boxed{P}$

Hence, option (a) is correct.

33. *(d)* As, $2+8=10$
Similarly, $6+3=9$
Hence, option (d) is correct.

34. *(d)* According to the question,

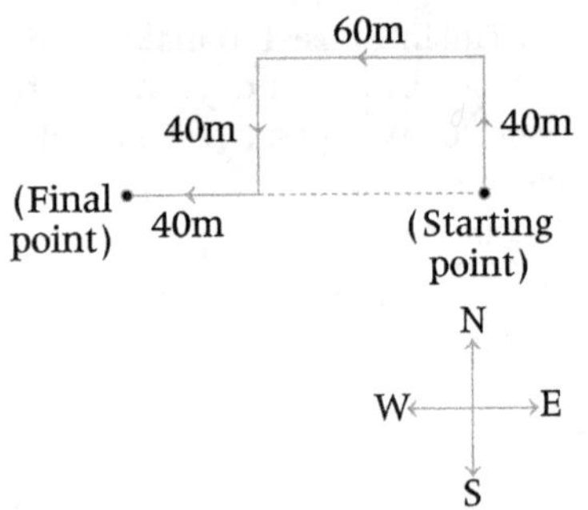

Distance between starting and final point
$= (60+40)\text{ m} = 100\text{ m}$
Hence, option (d) is correct.

35. *(d)* As,

R	E	S	A	N	O
+1↓	+1↓	+1↓	+1↓	+1↓	+1↓
S	1	T	2	O	3

Similarly,

M	O	R	A	L	E
+1↓	+1↓	+1↓	+1↓	+1↓	+1↓
N	3	S	2	M	1

Hence, option (d) is correct.

36. *(c)* There are three meaningful words are formed i.e. ARE, ATE, ART.
Hence, option (c) is correct.

37. *(b)* The water image of the given object is shown as,

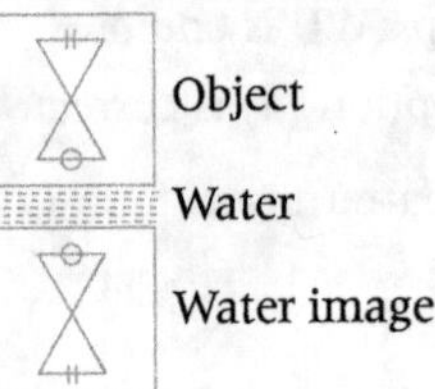

Hence, option (b) is correct.

38. *(d)* Number of students behind Nitin in rank
$=(49-18)=31$
So, Nitin is 32nd from the last.

39. *(c)* We have : $15\times2=30$, $2\times7=14$, $7\times9=63$.
So, missing number $=9\times15=135$

40. *(d)* The mirror image of the given word is as shown below:

FIXING | ƎNIXIF

Hence, option (d) is correct.

41. *(c)* On rearranging the letters given in options, we get

(a) MARCH (b) TODAY
(c) MONDAY (d) HOLIDAY

Among all these, only MONDAY is a day of a week.
Hence, option (c) is correct.

42. *(b)* The circle with shade and two dots, is rotating 90° in clockwise direction and the dot in square is moving one block in anti-clockwise direction in each step.
On following this pattern option figure (b) will come next.
Hence, option (b) is correct.

43. *(d)* When unfolding, the sheet will appear as

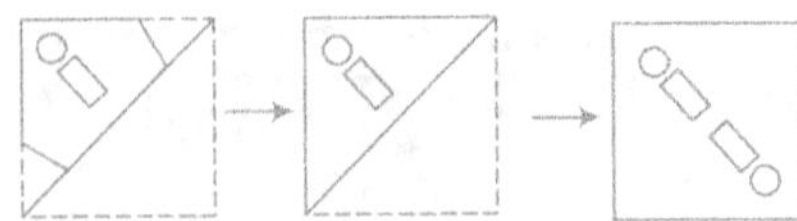

Hence, option (d) is correct.

44. *(b)* The give information can be represented as

Players	Cricket	Hockey	Chess	Swimming
Raghu	✓	✓	×	✓
Gyan	✓	✓	✓	×
Sohan	×	✓	✓	×
Govind	✓	×	×	✓

Clearly, Gyan is a good player in cricket, hockey and chess.

Hence, option (b) is correct.

45. *(c)* All the figures, except (c) are same when rotated but figure (c) is different.

So, figure (c) is odd one.

Hence, option (c) is correct.

46. *(d)* The female members in the family are mother, wives of 3 married sons, unmarried daughter and 2 daughters of each of the two sons.

∴ Number of female members

$= (1 + 3 + 1 + 2 \times 2)$

$= 9$

47. *(b)* According to the question,

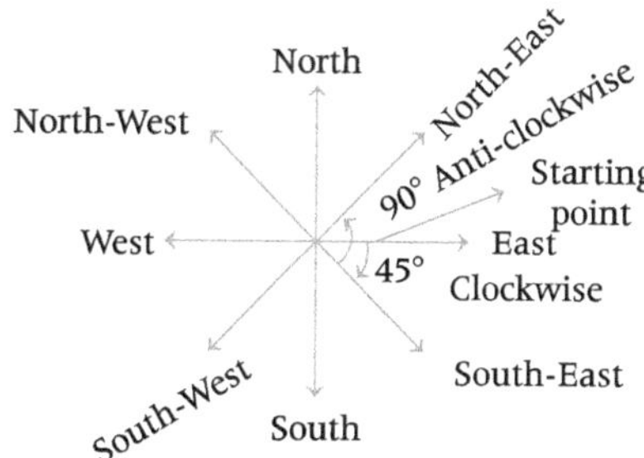

From the above diagram, it is clear that Rahul is facing toward North-East in his final position.

Hence, option (b) is correct.

48. *(a)* Here square is moving from one corner to another in anti-clockwise direction in each step but triangle changes its position diagonally in each alternate step.

On following this pattern, option figure (a) will complete the series.

Hence, option (a) is correct.

49. *(b)* On interchange '+' and '–', and '12' and '24' in option (b), we get the equation as:

$12 - 24 + 36 = 0$ or $24 + 12 - 36 = 0$

Which is true.

Hence, option (b) is correct.

50. *(d)* In each row, the third figure is the combination of the first and the second figure. On following this option figure (d) will replace the question mark.

Hence, option (d) is correct.

Practice Set-2

1. *(d)* According to the question ,

$D > M, W$ ...(i)

and $P > D, N$ ...(ii)

Here, the given information is not complete. So the given data is inadequate.

Hence, option (d) is correct.

2. *(c)* There are three 9's which immediately followed by an even number and preceded by and odd number

192 , 594 , 798

Hence, option (c) is correct.

3. *(c)* The mirror image of the given word is as shown below:

JUDGEMENT | TNEMEGDUJ

Mirror

Hence, option (c) is correct.

4. *(c)* The second is a class of the first and is available at the third.

5. *(d)* Option figure (d) contains figure (X).

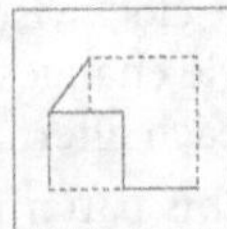

Hence, option (d) is correct.

6. *(c)* According to the question,

nice boy honest → eou geou quo ...(i)

nice state famous → quo you lou ...(ii)

From Eqs. (i) and (ii) 'nice' is common in both Eqs. (i) and (ii) so, the code for nice is 'quo'. Then, the code for 'nice is famous' is 'quo two muo'.

Hence, option (c) is correct.

7. *(d)* Here, all the digits of number have odd sum except option (d).

$3002 = 3 + 0 + 0 + 2 = 5;$

$4003 = 4 + 0 + 0 + 3 = 7;$

$5004 = 5 + 0 + 0 + 4 = 9$

But $6006 = 6 + 0 + 0 + 6 = 12$

So, 6006 is odd one.

Hence, option (d) is correct.

8. *(d)* On folding the given transparent sheet, we get

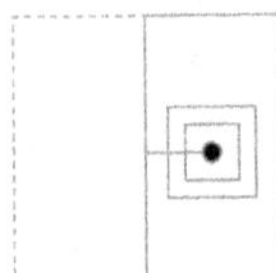

Hence, option (d) is correct.

9. *(a)* On applying the interchanges given in option (a), we get

LHS $= 52 + 38 - 88 = 90 - 88 = 2 =$ RHS

Hence,option (a) is correct.

10. *(a)* The given series can be represented as

$E \xrightarrow{+2} G \xrightarrow{+2} I \xrightarrow{+2} K \xrightarrow{+2} M$

$H \xrightarrow{+2} J \xrightarrow{+2} L \xrightarrow{+2} N \xrightarrow{+2} P$

$J \xrightarrow{-1} I \xrightarrow{-1} H \xrightarrow{-1} G \xrightarrow{-1} F$

Hence, option (a) is correct.

11. *(c)* The arrangement is :

$5 + 3 = 8,$

$8 + 4 = 12,$

$12 + 1 = 13.$

So, the missing number is 12.

12. *(d)* P's father is Q's son. So, Q is P's grandfather. M is the paternal uncle of P. So, M is the brother of P's father. This means that M is also Q's son. N is the brother of Q. Thus, N is the paternal uncle of P.

13. *(b)* We can understand clock problem by this diagram.

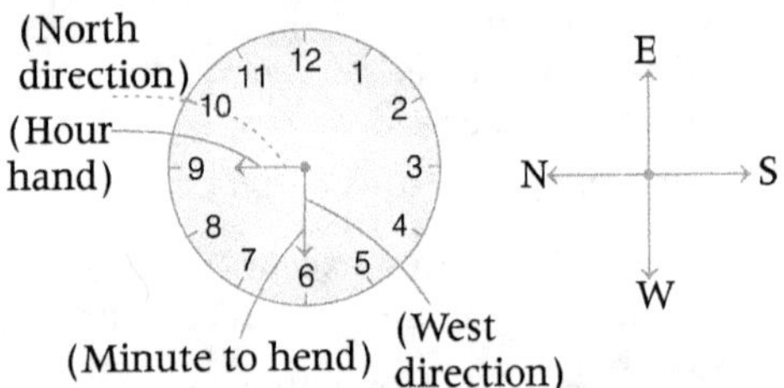

Form this minute hand is in West direction.

Hence, option (b) is correct.

14. *(d)* The water image of the given object is shown as below,

9 6 9

Water

Hence, option (d) is correct.

15. *(b)* $\because$ Price of 40 shirts $= ₹\ 1600$

$\therefore$ Price of 1 shirt $= \frac{1600}{40} = ₹\ 40$

$\therefore$ Price of 200 shirts will be $= ₹\ (40 \times 200)$

$= ₹\ 8000$

Hence, option (b) is correct.

16. *(d)* Except option (d), the sum of the positional value of given letter's is present in middle of the two letter.

$A + C = 1 + 3 = 4$

$D + G = 4 + 7 = 11$

$H + M = 8 + 13 = 21$

$Q + C = 17 + 3 \neq 19$

Here option (d) is odd. So, option (d) is correct.

17. *(a)*

18. *(d)* The mirror image of the given figure (X) is as shown below:

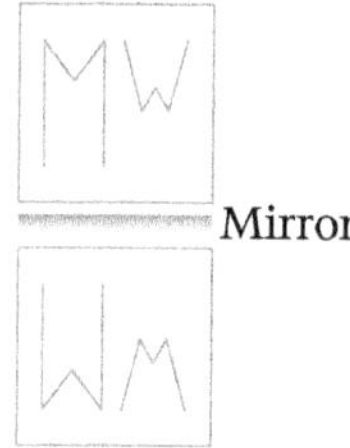

Hence, option (d) is correct.

19. *(b)* The water image of the given object is shown as below,

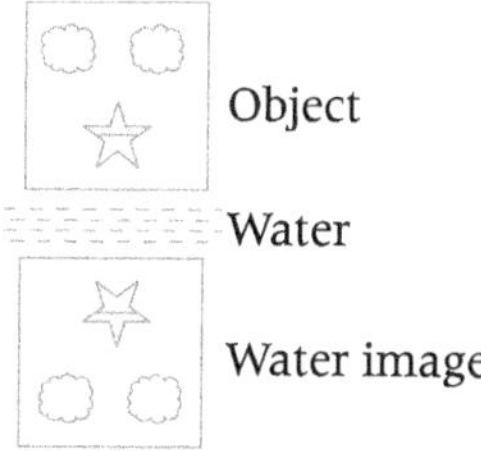

Hence, option (b) is correct.

20. *(a)* As explained above, B is the son of A and F is the spouse of A. So, B is the son of F.

21. *(b)* C is A's father's nephew means C is the son of A's father's brother i.e. C is the cousin of A. D is also A's cousin. So, D must be real brother or sister of C. But D is not brother of C. So, D must be sister of C.

22. *(d)* We have : $4 \times 2 - 1 = 7$, $7 \times 2 + 1 = 15$, $15 \times 2 - 1 = 29$

$$29 \times 2 + 1 = 59$$
$$59 \times 2 - 1 = 117$$
$$117 \times 2 + 1 = 235.$$

So missing number $= 235 \times 2 - 1 = 469.$

23. *(b)* Here, the figures are rotated with 90° in clockwise direction. So, the option (b) will be follow the same pattern.
Hence, option (b) is correct.

24. *(a)* The logical sequence of the words are infancy, childhood, puberty, Adulthood, senescence.

i.e. 2 4 1 3 5. Hence, option (a) is correct.

25. *(c)* On folding the given transparent sheet, we get

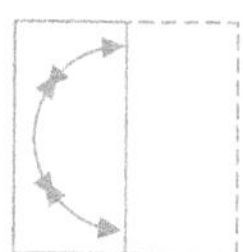

Hence, option (c) is correct.

26. *(a)* In block 1, 5, 7 figures have the same pattern.
In block 2, 6, 9 figures have the same pattern.
In block 3, 4, 8 figures have the same pattern.
So, the correct figure combinations are;
1, 5, 7; 2, 6, 9; 3, 4, 8
Hence, option (a) is correct.

27. *(c)* Here, the shaded portion is moving one step in anti-clockwise direction and dot changes its position diagonally in each successive step. On following this pattern option figure (c) will complete the series.

Hence, option (c) is correct.

28. *(b)* In the given coding system, we have

Letter	A	B	C	D	E	F	G	H
Code	3	5	7	9	11	13	15	17
Letter	I	J	K	L	M	N	O	P
Code	19	21	23	25	27	29	31	33

Here, we can see that, odd number values is the code for each letter.
So, 'MANGO' is coded as '273291531'
Similarly, 'PEA' is coded as '33113'.
Hence, option (b) is correct.

29. *(c)* According to the question,

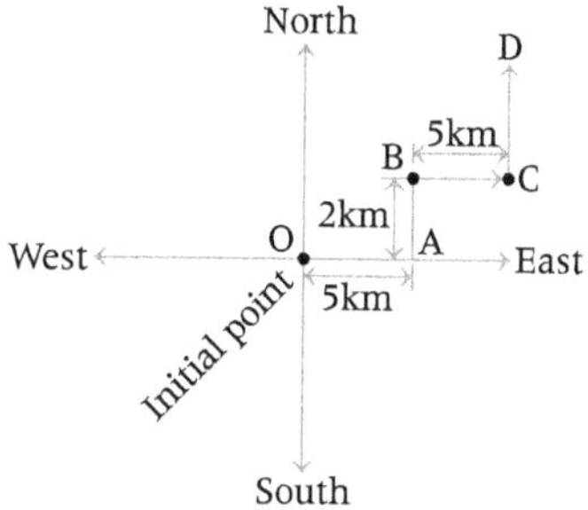

From the above figure, it is clear that he is facing in the North direction.

Hence, option (c) is correct.

30. *(b)* The sum of the two numbers in the upper part is 7 times the number in the lower part. So, missing number

$=(89+16)\div 7=15.$

31. *(d)* When unfolding, the sheet will appear as

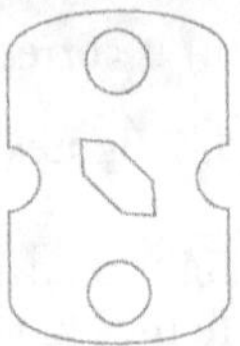

Hence, option (d) is correct.

32. *(c)* The words can be arranged as Afford, After, Answer, Avoid

Here, we see that, answer will come on second position from right side.

Hence, option (c) is correct.

33. *(b)* The mirror image of the given figure (X) is as shown below:

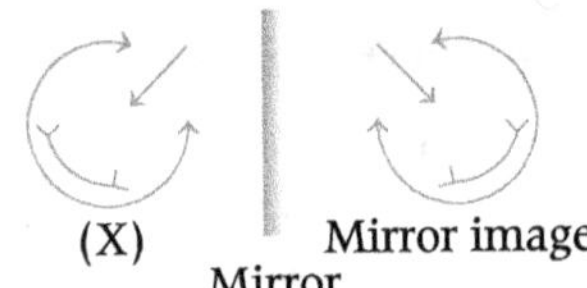

Hence, option (b) is correct.

34. *(c)* As,

D	A	R	E
+4 ↓	+4 ↓	+4 ↓	+4 ↓
H	E	V	I

Similarly,

M	A	I	N
+4 ↓	+4 ↓	+4 ↓	+4 ↓
Q	E	M	R

Hence, option (c) is correct.

35. *(c)* In all the figures except figure (c), the three white dots lie outside the main figure and one do tlies inside the main figure. But in figure (c) all the dots lies outside the main figure. So, option (c) is correct.

36. *(b)* By option (b) we have,

$10 > 4 \# 2 \& 6 > 8 < 2$

Now, on putting the values of symbols, we get.

$10\times 4+2<6\times 8-2 \Rightarrow 40+2<48-2$

$\Rightarrow 42<46$

So, 42 is less than 46.

Hence, option (b) is correct.

37. *(b)* Let A = 1, B = 2, C = 3, ..., W = 23, X = 24, Y = 25, Z = 26.

Then, $W-T=23-20=3;\ T-J=20-10=10,\ S-D=19-4=15$

So, missing number $= P-G = 16-7=9$

38. *(c)* According to the question,

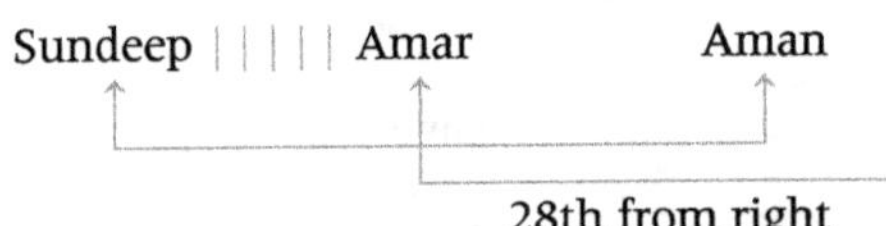

∴ Number of boys to the left of Sudeep

$=40-(28+6)$

$=40-34=6$

So, position of Aman from the left end

$=6+11=17\text{th}$

39. *(a)* There is only 'one' C's which is followed by D's but not preceded by E i.e.

E C D C E C D E E C D E D D C D E C E D C E

Hence, option (a) is correct.

40. *(c)* When unfolding, the sheet will appear as

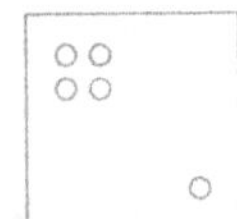

Hence, option (c) is correct.

Sol. (Q. Nos. 41 and 42) The given information can be analysed as under:

	Dramatics	Computer Science	Physics	History	Mathematics
A	✗	✓	✓	✓	✓
B	✓	✓	✓	✗	✗
C	✗	✗	✓	✓	✓
D	✓	✗	✓	✓	✗
E	✓	✓	✗	✓	✗

41. *(c)*

42. *(c)*

43. *(c)* According to the question,

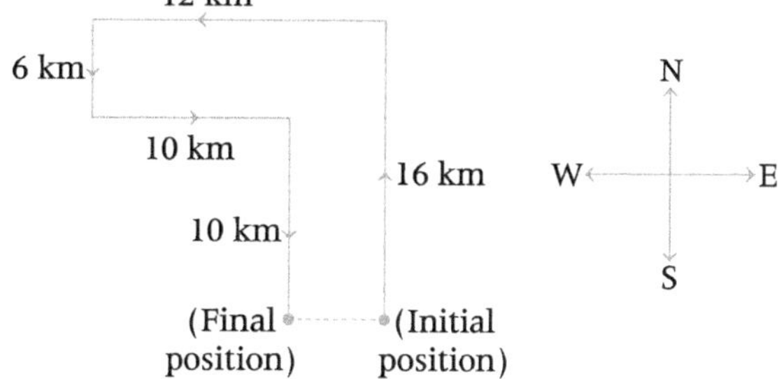

So, Sonia is 2 km, West from her starting point.

Hence, option (c) is correct.

44. *(a)* According to the question,

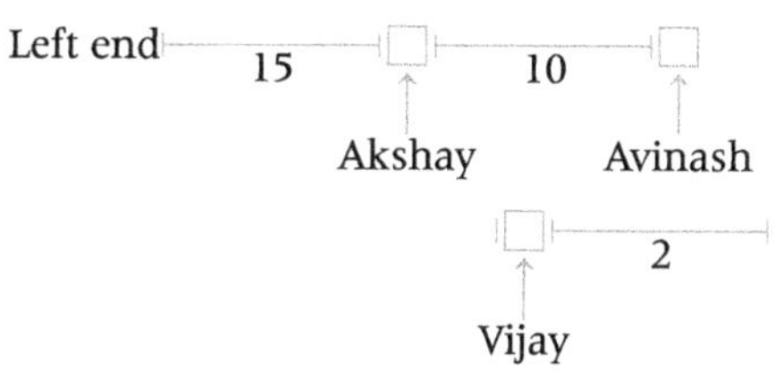

So, total number of boys $= 15 + 10 + 17 - 1$
$= 42 - 1 = 41$

Hence, option (a) is correct.

45. *(b)* 'MJEUZQN is coded as ' β&γ #+ >*'.

Hence, option (b) is correct.

46. *(d)* Code '<*#@>' is for the word 'TNUDQ'.

47. *(d)* As we move from figure (1) to figure (2), two line segments move one step in anti-clockwise direction and one line segment is added. While we move from figure (2) to figure (3), one line segment is deleted.

Following the similar pattern, we observe that figure (d) will be the next figure.

Hence, option (d) is correct.

48. *(d)* AS, place value of E is 5 in english Alphabetical order.

Place value of A is 1.

So, $5 + 1 = 6 = (6)^2 = 36$

and place value of C is 3.

place value of D is 4.

So, $3 + 4 = 7 = (7)^2 = 49$

Similarly, place value of E is 5.

Place value of F is 6.

So, $5 + 6 = 11 = (11)^2 = \boxed{121}$

Hence, option (d) is correct.

49. *(a)* We have, 14NO10LM42OP2MN6

On substitution the signs, we get,

$$14 \times 10 + 42 \div 2 - 6$$

Simplify the above expression using VBODMAS rule,

$$14 \times 10 + 42 \div 2 - 6$$
$$= 14 \times 10 + 21 - 6$$
$$= 140 + 21 - 6$$
$$= 161 - 6$$
$$= 155$$

Hence, option (a) is correct.

50. *(b)*

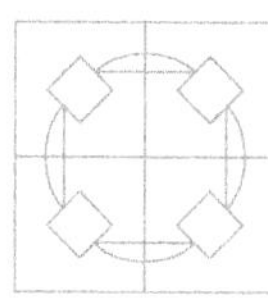

Hence, option (b) is correct.

www.ingramcontent.com/pod-product-compliance
Lightning Source LLC
LaVergne TN
LVHW080043170826
845677LV00024B/1425

* 9 7 8 9 3 2 5 5 1 9 0 5 3 *